FROM PROVO TO PAKISTAN

FLOODING THE EARTH WITH THE BOOK OF MORMON

an inspiring true story

BY SEAN DIXON & STEPHEN ANJUM
WITH STEPHAN TAEGER

CFI
An imprint of Cedar Fort, Inc.
Springville, Utah

© 2025 Sean Dixon, Stephen Anjum, and Stephan Taeger
All rights reserved.

No part of this book may be reproduced in any form whatsoever, whether by graphic, visual, electronic, film, microfilm, tape recording, or any other means, without prior written permission of the publisher, except in the case of brief passages embodied in critical reviews and articles.

This is not an official publication of The Church of Jesus Christ of Latter-day Saints. The opinions and views expressed herein belong solely to the author and do not necessarily represent the opinions or views of Cedar Fort, Inc. Permission for the use of sources, graphics, and photos is also solely the responsibility of the author.

Paperback ISBN 13: 978-1-4621-4945-2
eBook ISBN 13: 978-1-4621-4946-9

Published by CFI, an imprint of Cedar Fort, Inc.
2373 W. 700 S., Suite 100, Springville, UT 84663
Distributed by Cedar Fort, Inc., www.cedarfort.com

Library of Congress Control Number: 2025936330

Cover design by Shawnda Craig
Cover design © 2025 Cedar Fort, Inc.
Edited and Typeset by Liz Kazandzhy

Printed in the United States of America

10 9 8 7 6 5 4 3 2 1

Printed on acid-free paper

To M'Shelle, my partner every step of the way!

-Sean

To my mother, Shanti — your voice led me
to Christ and a lifelong mission.

-Stephen

To Scott Anderson

-Stephan

CONTENTS

Introduction 1

1 A Letter from the Other Side of the World 3

2 Sean's Conversion 6

3 The Book's Journey 11

4 Growing Up in Pakistan 16

5 Sharing the Good News 23

6 Resolving Concerns in Toronto 28

7 Seeking For the Church 32

8 Thomsena 40

9 Meeting M'Shelle 47

10 Establishing the Church 51

11 Razzaq Gill and Three Copies of the Book of Mormon 57

12 The Ways We Gather: Love, Share, Invite 62

13 London, England 69

14 A New Life in England 79

15 Let the Book Speak for Itself 84

16 The Reunion 90

Epilogue 95

Appendix 96

About the Authors 143

Introduction

I first heard the account of Stephen Anjum when I observed my colleague Sean Dixon teach a class at the Utah Valley Institute. As I listened to him relate the true story of a Pakistani man encountering the Book of Mormon, I felt like Jeremiah: "Mine heart [was] as a burning fire shut up in my bones" (Jeremiah 20:9). I approached Sean after class and told him I was deeply inspired by the lesson. The next day, he emailed me and asked if I would help write a book about Stephen's experience.

This story is a true parable. It is a factual account that teaches profound truths. Inside these pages, you will read an astonishing account that witnesses of the power of the Book of Mormon, the Lord's desire to gather people from every nation, and the Christ-centered friendships that can develop across borders and cultures. Truly this is a story of miracles. While this narrative shares Stephen's experience and that of his close associates, we also acknowledge the contributions and sacrifice of many other early Pakistani saints not mentioned in this book.

While this account focuses on Sean Dixon and Stephen Anjum, it has been written in Sean's voice. However, Stephen played an essential role in helping craft this story. He provided the details for the events related to his life, and gratefully, Stephen's own words are also present in the letters that are included throughout the book.

Our prayer is that you will be motivated by Stephen's story to use the Book of Mormon to gather Israel. In the words of President Ezra Taft Benson, "Combined with the Spirit of the Lord, the Book of Mormon is the greatest single tool which God has given us to convert the world."[1]

Stephan Taeger

"I challenge our Church writers, teachers, and leaders to tell us more Book of Mormon conversion stories that will strengthen our faith and prepare great missionaries. Show us how to effectively use it as a missionary tool, and let us know how it leads us to Christ and answers our personal problems and those of the world."

—President Ezra Taft Benson[2]

---

1. Ezra Taft Benson, "A New Witness for Christ," *Ensign*, Nov. 1984, 7.

2. Ezra Taft Benson, "Flooding the World with the Book of Mormon," *Ensign*, Nov. 1988, 5.

1

A Letter from the Other Side of the World

Spring 1989

"Sean, who do you know in Pakistan?" my mom said as I entered through the front door of our white, split-level home in Provo, Utah.

I laughed and said, "Nobody. Why do you ask?"

"I got the most interesting letter from the mailbox today."

She held up an envelope that had three large stamps from Pakistan and a postmark from a place called Faisalabad. My name and address were written neatly in red ink on the front.

Intrigued, I took the envelope from her hand, wondering who would be writing *me* a letter from across the world.

I was eighteen years old, finishing my first year as a student at Utah Valley State College and working as a waiter at Magleby's restaurant to try to earn money for my upcoming mission to Toronto, Canada. We lived in one of those idyllic middle-class neighborhoods situated against the hills on the northeast side of Provo. To this day, I have never found a sledding hill that matches the one directly behind my house. I grew up with four siblings and about twenty boys my age in my ward. Our red brick church was a block from our house, and there was a park across the street where I played basketball, football, baseball, and every night game imaginable. I was raised with the gospel of Jesus Christ, family, friends, and sports at the center of my life. Those foundational days of my adolescence were quickly ending as I anticipated leaving for Canada in the coming weeks.

I anxiously opened the letter and was introduced to my new friend Stephen Anjum. The letter read:

> Dear Sean,
>
> My name is Stephen Anjum and I am a Pakistani Christian. Some times ago I came to know about you and, (the Book of Mormon) Another Testament of Jesus Christ. I went through the Holy book and found that this is real book of God. I believe that Mormon church is true and I also believe that Joseph Smith was a True Prophet of God. I believe that it is a gift of God. I hope that anyone, who will read it and pray will get blessing of God.
>
> Dear Sean, I wish to be preacher of Holy Mormon. I want to get more knowledge about Mormon. Please send me some books in easy English related to Mormons. If you have any representative in Pakistan then inform me so that I may get more information from him. I hope you will accept my friendship.
>
> YOUR BROTHER IN CHRIST,
> Stephen Anjum

I was surprised, excited, and overwhelmed by the letter. I reread the phrase, "If you have any representative in Pakistan then inform me so that I can get more information from him." I wondered, "Who is this man? How does he know me? And how does he have my address?" I had no idea what to do about the letter, but I sensed how important it was that I got it into the right hands.

"Sean, run down to the Milletts' house and talk to Brother Millett," my mom suggested. "He works for the missionary department, and he'll know what to do."

I went down the street with the letter in hand and eagerly knocked on his door. Brother Millett invited me into his home, and I showed him the letter. After he read it, he was taken aback and asked how Stephen knew me and how a copy of the Book of Mormon could have made it all the way to Pakistan, a country where the Church did not have a presence.

"I don't know," I shrugged. "Can you help me? What should I do next?"

After thinking about it, he recommended a plan for each of us. He told me to write Stephen and teach him all that I could about the gospel of Jesus Christ by letter. I was to become his pen pal. Brother Millett would inform Church leaders so that they could contact the Area Presidency over that part of the world. They, in turn, would put Stephen in contact with the nearest member of the Church.

Although I didn't feel adequate for the task, we both went to work, eager to find a way to bring the restored gospel to this seeker of truth.

2

SEAN'S CONVERSION

STEPHEN'S LETTER CAME AT AN EXCITING TIME FOR ME. WITH ONLY about a month left until I entered the missionary training center, I was on fire with the gospel of Jesus Christ. I related to Stephen when he said that he had gone through the Book of Mormon and found that it was real and that the Church was true and Joseph Smith was a prophet of God. I even identified with his unique statement that he wished "to be preacher of Holy Mormon." I was eager to go on my mission to share the truths that had transformed my life. But that was not always the case.

I was raised an active member of the Church in a strong Latter-day Saint family. However, in my early teenage years, my membership was merely cultural. I was driven by external expectations and not by an inner conversion. I had a natural inclination to follow rules and go with the flow but was not yet seeking a testimony of my own.

For most of my growing up, my dad was either in the bishopric in our home ward or serving as a bishop in a young adult ward on the campus of Brigham Young University (BYU). As a young deacon, I remember passing the sacrament once a month to the college students in the ward where my dad served as bishop. He was a social worker by profession, and because our family was on a tight budget, he taught me the importance of challenging work and encouraged me to get jobs to pay for the extra things I wanted. He was someone I could talk to about anything and was a notable example of living the gospel, but he didn't push me to study and ask tough questions. He expressed love freely and supported me in anything I cared about.

During that time, I also shared a room with my brother, Scott, who was eight years older than me. Scott was one of the star athletes in his high school and my hero. I wanted to be like him in every way, even though I was annoyed when he kept the light on at night while he read the Book of Mormon. At the time, I didn't understand why reading the Book of Mormon mattered so much to him.

Almost all my neighbors were members of the Church, and for most of my childhood, it didn't occur to me to question whether the Church was true. It was simply the only church I knew.

When I was about fourteen years old, something happened that began to change me. I accepted a challenge to read the Book of Mormon every day. I did so mostly because that was what everyone at church was asked to do, not because of any quest for truth. But when I began to read, I found that I enjoyed the book. I liked the stories and how I felt when I read, even though I didn't see what was happening to me. I plugged away for many months and finally came to the promise found in Moroni 10. After reading the book for nearly a year, I decided it would be good to pray about its truthfulness. I believed the promise and decided to kneel and put Moroni to the test. I expected a powerful spiritual experience like I heard about in testimony meetings. I asked. I waited. I listened. But nothing happened. I continued to read and pray, and each time, I was disappointed. Where was my spiritual experience? Would I have to do what Enos did and pray all day and all night?

Finally, one night as I prayed, a thought entered my mind: "Think about what has happened to your life since you started reading the Book of Mormon." I pondered on that and recalled who I used to be and who I had become.

I remembered a boy in my ward who was constantly teased and belittled. I remember standing by, grateful that it wasn't me. That was before the Book of Mormon. I realized now that I felt offended when I saw someone treated poorly. I found myself befriending and defending them. That was a notable change. I remembered the off-color jokes that used to amuse me. That was before the Book of Mormon. Now they weren't funny. I remember being bored at church, trying to endure it. That was before the Book of Mormon. Now I enjoyed church and had become interested in learning doctrine. The gospel was coming alive for me that year, and I hadn't even noticed.

When I looked back, I saw a remarkable difference: I was being born again. I felt like King Benjamin's people when they described themselves after his powerful sermon. They said God had "wrought a mighty change in [them], or in [their] hearts, that [they had] no more disposition to do evil, but to do good continually" (Mosiah 5:2) The Spirit came over me, and I knew the Book of Mormon was true. Not due to a single moment but because of how my spiritual life had been ignited. I can trace my conversion to Jesus Christ and His gospel to the day I began my quest to study the Book of Mormon. I have never been the same.

With this flame of faith inside me, I could tell others from my own changed heart that the book was of God. Now I understood why my brother Scott kept the light on! From that point forward, my efforts to live the gospel were my own, and I was excited for the day I could serve a mission. With my testimony firmly in place, I began to have a variety of new experiences with the Book of Mormon.

President Ezra Taft Benson was the prophet of my teenage years. He is remembered for many things but perhaps most of all for his emphasis on the Book of Mormon. For example, in one of his famous talks, he urged members of the Church to "flood the earth" with the Book of Mormon: "We have the Book of Mormon, we have the members, we have the missionaries, we have the resources, and the world has the need. The time is now! . . . Indeed, I have a vision of flooding the earth with the Book of Mormon."[3]

During my senior year, in response to the call of our prophet, the seminary council at Timpview High School created an after-school missionary activity based on an initiative by the Church called the "Family to Family Book of Mormon" program. Students who wanted

---

3. Ezra Taft Benson, "Flooding the Earth with the Book of Mormon," *Ensign*, Nov. 1988, 3.

CHAPTER 2: SEAN'S CONVERSION

to participate purchased a copy of the Book of Mormon and then personalized it by writing their testimony and return address on one of the beginning pages. The seminary teachers told us they would gather the books and take them to Church headquarters where the Church would distribute them to full-time missionaries.

Of course, I gladly purchased and personalized a book and dropped it in a basket, but I didn't think anything more about it, as I had previously participated in other "Family to Family Book of Mormon" events like this one. If only I had known then what would become of it.

While I was attending my first year of college, I had an opportunity to fly to Miami, Florida, with my family to watch my brother-in-law Lee Johnson play in the Super Bowl. He was the punter for the Cincinnati Bengals, and they were playing the San Francisco 49ers. As a big football fan, I couldn't wait to go to this once-in-a-lifetime game. Just before leaving on the trip, my mission prep teacher gave each of us a copy of the Book of Mormon and invited us to prayerfully give it away. I was determined to find someone I could share my copy with on the way to Miami.

As the flight was nearing completion, I noticed a legendary NFL wide receiver sitting four or five rows in front of me. The thought came into my mind, "Share your book with him." I immediately became fearful and thought of all the reasons I couldn't do that, but I remembered he was a Christian, and the thought persisted. So I wrote my testimony inside the front cover. I told him how much I respected him and how I wanted to share this with him. Then I signed my name, wrapped it in paper, and approached him. I asked him for his autograph and then told him I had something for him. I quickly handed the Book of Mormon over and bolted back to my seat. I was relieved that I had done my duty and was glad I didn't need to talk to him or answer any questions.

Looking back on that day, I realize my goal was focused on just getting that book to someone rather than really helping them want to read it. My desire to share the gospel and the Book of Mormon was strong, but my confidence in doing so was lacking. Despite my awkward attempt, I went back to my seat filled with joy at having tried to do my best to be an instrument in the hands of God. I looked forward to the time when the opportunity would arise again.

Before leaving on that trip to Miami, I filled out my mission papers and turned them in to my stake president, Carl Bacon, who lived next door. I was eager to get home to find out where I would be serving.

One morning, President Bacon's son Ken, who was my close friend, pounded on my door and told me my call was in the mailbox! I ran outside, retrieved the letter, and went to show it to my mom, who was the only one home. She coaxed me to open it right then and there without waiting.

She asked me where I thought I would be going. President Bacon and his family had recently returned home from serving as the mission president in Toronto, Canada. Ken told me all about it, and I thought that it would be an amazing place to serve. So when my mom asked, I said, "I think it'll be the Canada Toronto Mission." She told me she thought I would go Spanish-speaking.

I opened the call, and to our amazement, it said I was called to serve in the Canada Toronto Mission. Plus, I would learn the discussions in Spanish! My excitement to serve and the feeling that God knew me reached an all-time high.

A couple of months later, the letter from Stephen Anjum came to that same mailbox. The Lord was going to make me an instrument in His hands much sooner than I expected.

3
THE BOOK'S JOURNEY

THE DAY I RECEIVED THE LETTER FROM PAKISTAN, MY MIND CENtered on two questions. First, who was Stephen Anjum? And second, how did he come to know about me and the Book of Mormon?

I followed Brother Millett's suggestion and wrote a letter to Stephen. I was in a missionary preparation class at the time, so I was happy to put into practice what I was learning. I introduced myself, expressed my gratitude at receiving his letter, and then proceeded to share an overview of the first missionary discussion with him. I explained that we would try to put him in contact with a member of the Church in Pakistan as soon as possible. I also told him I would continue to share further information about the Church. Of course, my central question was to know more about his story, how he had received the Book of Mormon, and how he knew about me. I sealed the envelope and sent it to his mailing address in Pakistan, which was at his father's place of work.

Time passed and eventually his second letter arrived. In the letter, Stephen described himself as a twenty-four-year-old Pakistani Christian. He was from a family of ten children. His mother died when he was eighteen, and his father was working for a local bank. He explained that only 2 percent of the population in Pakistan were

Christian, while approximately 97 percent were Muslim. Stephen had recently graduated from Government College University in Pakistan and taught science at a high school. In the letter, he said, "Yes, of course, 'the Mormon Book' has a great influence on me and I love it so much. You will be pleased that I have introduced this book to my best friends. My friends also show their strong interest in this church."

My curiosity about how Stephen got the book and how it was connected to me was overwhelming. I couldn't wait to solve the mystery.

Over time, I was able to piece together what happened. In the late 1980s, a young Pakistani man had the desire to become a Christian minister. Since Pakistan is predominantly a Muslim nation, there were few opportunities for training near the minister's home. He decided to travel to Bristol, England, to attend a Christian seminary where he could prepare himself for the ministry and return to his country to start his own church. One day, while on the streets of Bristol, he met two missionaries for The Church of Jesus Christ of Latter-day Saints. They gave him a personalized copy of the Book of Mormon and invited him to read it. The young man took the book back to the seminary and asked his trainers what they thought of the book. They told him it was an evil book and that he should warn the world about it and the Church the book represented. When the young aspiring pastor completed his training in England, he was determined to return to his country, follow their counsel, and warn others about the Book of Mormon.

When the pastor arrived in Pakistan, he worked hard to establish his own church. One day, the pastor's younger brother approached his close college friend, Stephen Anjum, and invited him to attend a new church where his brother would be preaching a sermon against "a disgusting book" from America called the Book of Mormon. Stephen agreed to attend and listened attentively to the pastor's words.

After the sermon, Stephen approached his friend and asked him if he or his brother had read the Book of Mormon. When he replied in the negative, Stephen asked if he could borrow the book from him. The pastor agreed, and the next day, Stephen's friend gave him the book.

Originally, Stephen's desire was to use the book to study English, but when he read the cover—*The Book of Mormon: Another Testament*

12

of Jesus Christ—he felt the Holy Ghost whisper to him that this was a very special book. Despite the warnings from the young pastor, Stephen could sense that what he was saying was not right. Rather than simply accept the pastor's word, Stephen let the book speak for itself. When he opened it and began to read, he described his initial experience this way:

> I read about Lehi and his children wandering in the desert and about them ending up in the New World. I thought, this was a great thing, Jesus Christ and Heavenly Father must have gave us this book. We are children of God, and if the Bible was an account of his children in the Eastern Hemisphere, there must be children of God in other parts of the world.

His desire to use the book to learn English quickly faded, and he began to read it with real intent. For the next two months (June and July 1988), Stephen studied the Book of Mormon, trying to discover its purpose. He wanted to know which church it came from and who authored it. One night as he was studying and praying, he received a witness from the Holy Ghost that it was a true book from God. As Stephen looked through it more closely, he noticed a piece of paper that was glued to the front of the book. On the paper, he found my testimony about the truthfulness of the book and the Prophet Joseph Smith written in red cursive handwriting. The note also contained my return address in Utah.

The Book of Mormon did its own heavy lifting with Stephen Anjum. His only introduction to the book was that it was "disgusting" and to beware of it, yet he only had to read the title to feel the Holy Ghost whisper that it was special. As he continued to read, the book's power became evident, and he received the witness confirming that it was indeed true.

Armed with a testimony of the truthfulness of the Book of Mormon, Stephen returned to the pastor to talk to him about what he found in the book. He asked the pastor if he knew where the people associated with the Book of Mormon were from. Concerned, the pastor asked Stephen if he was interested in the book. Stephen replied that it was an inspiring book that spoke of Jesus Christ. Frustrated that his efforts to warn the Pakistani people about the evils of the

Book of Mormon had backfired with Stephen, the pastor sent his brother to ask for the book back. Before Stephen returned the book, he quickly turned to the front page and wrote down my name and address. From then on, he searched for the church that was associated with the book. He told his father, Barkat Benedict, about his curiosity about the book and asked him for help typing a letter to me on his old typewriter. That letter is the one that my mom retrieved from the mailbox on that spring day in 1989.

As I pondered the mystery, I realized that one of the books I had sent out as part of the "Family to Family Book of Mormon" program must have made it all the way to England and then on to Pakistan. I have reflected many times on the journey of that copy of the Book of Mormon: from my hand to Church headquarters, to the mission office in England, into the hands of two missionaries in Bristol, into the hands and suitcase of the pastor, and from there to Stephen Anjum in Pakistan. The Lord does what is needed to gather scattered Israel, even if He must fly the Book of Mormon to Pakistan in the suitcase of an antagonist of the Church!

Having lost his only copy of the Book of Mormon, Stephen wrote that first letter and later requested that I send a new copy of the Book of Mormon and Bible. I prepared a package with several copies of the Book of Mormon—personalized by my family and neighbors—and the rest of the standard works: the Bible, Doctrine and Covenants, and Pearl of Great Price. I also included *A Marvelous Work and a Wonder* and the *Gospel Principles* manual. We mailed them off and Stephen received them with excitement.

Later from Toronto, I sent another box to Stephen with more copies of the Book of Mormon. Now Stephen had several copies of the book to share with those who expressed interest.

As I learned Stephen's story, I shared it with Brother Richard Millett. He told Church leadership in Salt Lake about the letter I received, and in response, Elder Russell Taylor, the assistant director of the missionary department, wrote a letter that reached the Area Presidency in Hong Kong, China. At that time, Hong Kong was the headquarters of the area of the Church that encompassed Pakistan.

CHAPTER 3: THE BOOK'S JOURNEY

Now, in addition to my correspondence with Stephen, the Area Presidency was busy looking for ways to connect him with a representative of the Church.

4

GROWING UP IN PAKISTAN

As Stephen was learning more about the gospel, I wanted to know all I could about him. I took Brother Millett's suggestion to become Stephen's pen pal seriously, and the two of us corresponded over the years. As my friendship with Stephen Anjum grew, I realized how strikingly different our life experiences were, and yet there were also some unexpected similarities. I learned that he experienced poverty and devastating loss in Pakistan in a way I couldn't imagine in my sheltered life in Provo.

It wasn't until years later that Stephen shared with me the story of his youth. As I listened to him recount the details of his past, my compassion and understanding of who he really was and how God was preparing him began to deepen. The following is a little of what I have learned about my friend.

Stephen was born on October 6, 1963, in Rahim Yar Khan, Pakistan. He was the eldest of ten children born to Barkat Benedict and Shanti Cecilia. According to Pakistani custom, Shanti went to Rahim Yar Khan to be with her mother for the birth of Stephen, and his father Barkat remained behind in Faisalabad to work.

One night, while alone and away from his wife, Stephen's father had a dream. In the dream, he was told that a baby boy would be born, his name should be Stephen, and there would be a birthmark on his left leg. Barkat prayerfully reflected on the dream and wrote a letter to his father-in-law, Manohar Lal, saying that if a baby boy was born, they should name him Stephen Anjum and check for a birthmark on his left leg.

When Manohar Lal received the letter, he kept it in mind. After the baby's birth, a red birthmark was indeed visible on his left leg. Everyone was amazed at how Barkat Benedict had known this in advance. At the time, Shanti was unwell, so Manohar Lal asked his niece, Martha, to take the baby to a nearby photo studio. A picture of baby Stephen was taken with his aunt Martha. Manohar Lal then sent the photograph to his son-in-law, Barkat, along with a letter expressing his surprise and amazement at how he had known about the birthmark beforehand.

Prior to giving birth to Stephen, Shanti went to a church in Multan and, much like Hannah in the Old Testament, prayed to God and pleaded that if the Lord would bless her with a son, she would devote him to the church.

Stephen came from a long line of Christian ancestors, which is rare in Pakistan. His paternal grandfather, Francis Achar, was a medic in the British Indian Army in World War II. His family was Catholic long before the partition in 1947 when Pakistan became a country and broke off from India for religious purposes. His maternal grandfather, Manohar Lal, was the only educated person among his siblings and became a prominent leader of his Christian community in Rahim Yar Khan. He was also a senior officer in the Deputy Commissioner's office in that city. Barkat and Shanti were optimistic that their son would carry on this rich family tradition of community service and faith.

Similarly, I often heard my parents talking about our faithful pioneer ancestors on both sides of the family. I will never forget learning about the conversion story of Henry Aldous Dixon in South Africa or how Joseph Leland Heywood was baptized in the Mississippi River after Joseph Smith cut a hole in the ice with his own axe. I will always remember that Miles Romney supervised the construction of the St. George Temple and tabernacle, and James Henrie was in the vanguard pioneer company with Brigham Young. It was clear that my parents shared these stories to instill in me a sense of gratitude for those who had sacrificed so much for me to have the gospel of Jesus Christ. Like Stephen's parents, my mom and dad wanted me to follow in their footsteps.

Stephen grew up in a poor area in Faisalabad that was near his father's place of work at the Standard Chartered Bank. While I sledded in the hills behind my house and played sports in the park across the street, he played in a nearby canal that was in between his house and the Catholic church he attended. His dad's sister Clara left the convent where she had been a nun for eight years and moved in with the family. She was strict and took it upon herself to teach the children a very rigid form of Catholicism.

Stephen remembers at age ten hearing the church bells ring followed by the demands of his aunt for them to go to church. She wasn't above corporal punishment to make sure they lived up to her strict religious guidelines. In those days, his experience with church was not pleasant. However, over time he developed friendships with other boys going to church, and his feelings about his faith began to improve. All the boys looked forward to the time they could become altar boys. When Stephen's time arrived to be an altar boy, he was shy and nervous to have people watch him perform his duties, but in time he became more comfortable. I felt some of those same feelings when passing the sacrament to my dad's BYU ward when I was twelve.

In addition to participating in communion and the sacrament in similar and yet diverse ways, both Stephen and I received religious education during our school years. While I took seminary classes in high school, his religious upbringing included education at a Catholic school called Lasalle.

Near Stephen's home, there was a transport station where many people came from distant places. This sometimes brought a rough crowd to Faisalabad, and there were stories told of children being kidnapped and taken to foreign countries. This created a lot of fear and anxiety for Stephen as a boy when he needed to be in town. To cope with the worry, he developed the practice of singing aloud a Christian song in Urdu called "I Will Go from Home to Home and Preach the Gospel of Jesus Christ." He said this song brought him comfort and

CHAPTER 4: GROWING UP IN PAKISTAN

chased away his fears. It also foreshadowed what was to come later in his life.

Despite his Aunt Clara's strict and sometimes heavy approach, she taught him many foundational principles that blessed his life. For example, she taught him that you could always tell if someone was a Christian because they would talk about three things: God, Jesus Christ as the Son of God, and the Holy Ghost.

He never forgot this lesson, and when he first started reading the Book of Mormon, he was looking to see if the book talked about each member of the Godhead. He was immediately delighted to see that the Book of Mormon was a Christian book. In addition, the Anjum family also gathered each night to pray. To this day, Stephen still remembers Psalm 23 word for word, which he was asked to memorize and recite regularly. Those inspiring words of the Psalm brought him great comfort and strength in the coming years when he would have to face heart-wrenching trials.

Eventually, Barkat Benedict was able to get a construction loan from the bank where he worked so that he could move his family to a better part of the city called Warispura. Barkat was a hardworking man who labored day and night to provide for his family. He was not home much, but he did the best he could to make sure his family's needs were met.

In January 1982, when Stephen was eighteen, the family (consisting of ten children) was living in their new home, which was still under construction. At that time, the home had two rooms and no heat or electricity. It was in this home that a tragedy occurred that would forever affect the rest of Stephen's life.

On a wintry night when Barkat was away in Lahore for work, Stephen heard his mother screaming out in pain in the adjoining room. Leaving his nine siblings in the other room, Stephen ran to his mother, only to find that her health was in serious trouble. She told him that it felt like her legs were being stabbed by knives. She told Stephen that an untrained nurse, which Stephen called a witch doctor, had come to give her a procedure. It did not go well, and her body was having an extreme reaction.

Stephen got on the family motorcycle and went frantically searching for a doctor. He found a doctor who told him about an injection

19

his mother could receive, but Stephen would have to find it in a pharmacy. Stephen sped around the city as fast as he could but could never find the injection. He hurried home and found his mother's situation desperate. At 5 a.m., he rented a rickshaw to take his crying mother five kilometers to the nearest hospital. When the doctors saw her condition, they wondered why she had not come to the hospital for the procedure. They gave her medication for the pain, but it soon became clear that she was dying. Stephen sat with his mother, providing her comfort.

When the bell rang indicating visiting hours were over, Stephen was excused from the room. However, as he walked away, he knew that might be the last time he would see his mother. So he ignored the rule and went back to be by Shanti's side. He told her he was praying for her and that he knew she would get well.

She looked at him with penetrating eyes and told him she was dying and that she wanted him to do two things. First, she told him that he needed to press forward and get his education. She had only a primary education, but knew how important it was he become an educated man. Second, she asked him to look out for his brothers and sisters. Those final requests were riveted into his soul. Stephen assured her that he would do those two things. That promise to his dying thirty-six-year-old mother helped shape the rest of his life.

Barkat was able to come to his wife's side and she died shortly afterward. While experiencing tremendous grief, Stephen was left with the enormous responsibility of looking after his nine siblings and figuring out his education.

Stephen said that this traumatic experience with his mother gave him a deep sense of humility, compassion, and responsibility. It drew him closer to God as he constantly pleaded for the strength and ability to do what he needed to do. He never blamed God for what happened. Instead, he pressed forward in Christ.

Two years later, in 1984, Stephen received more tragic news. His father was involved in a bus accident and his leg was fractured. Stephen rode his motorcycle to the hospital to find Barkat severely injured. A doctor performed surgery, and screws were inserted in his leg to hold the bones together. Unfortunately, the screws caused a severe infection that left him disabled for the next six years. He had three bone grafts in those years, and Stephen and his siblings were left to care for their disabled father. Stephen had to nurse his father's wounds and attend to his daily needs.

During that time, Stephen never forgot his mother's dying words that he needed to pursue an education. While taking care of his dad and attending to his responsibilities at home, he applied for admission to Government College University. He was quickly rejected. Although profoundly disappointed, he did not give up. Stephen inquired at the university, and he was referred to the director of admissions. As the two met, Stephen showed the professor his dad's X-rays and told him that his father had been involved in a serious accident and that he had been caring for him for the past year. Due to this, despite getting good grades and meeting the admission requirements, the forms were not filled out on time. Stephen pleaded for an exception and let the professor know how important getting into college was for his future. The professor was stern and excused Stephen from the room, telling him there was nothing he could do and that Stephen would not be admitted. Stephen left the room dejected, got on his bicycle, and rode home to his family brokenhearted.

After a week, and remembering his promise to his mother, Stephen asked his father to pray for him and to ask the Lord to bless him with a way to get admitted. His father gave a heartfelt prayer and Stephen returned to the campus and walked around wondering what to do. He felt desperate and lost but hopeful that his father's prayer would be answered and a solution could be found. Miraculously, some students approached him while he wandered around and told him the registrar wanted to see him immediately.

Stephen nervously went back into the office of the director of admissions and was greeted by an entirely different countenance. The professor told him that for the entire week, he had felt vexed by how he had treated Stephen and had been looking out the window for him to return. Immediately after he excused Stephen, he realized his mistake and lack of compassion and sent people looking for him, but he had already gone home. He kept his eyes open and had excitedly seen Stephen through the window that day. He apologized and asked him what degree he wanted to pursue. Stephen said he wanted a bachelor's degree in science so he could teach mathematics and other subjects.

His admission was immediately granted. His father's humble prayer was answered. As he told me this intense story of pursuing his education, I realized that I had taken for granted the straightforward process of applying for and gaining admission to BYU.

One day, during his studies, Stephen shared with me that he became extremely stressed. He had a major exam to take to receive his bachelor's degree, but he did not feel prepared due to his many responsibilities at home. At the peak of his worry, he looked up and saw a picture of Jesus Christ. He knelt in front of the picture and began to pour out his heart to God. He asked for God's help to carry him through and to help him with the test. He got up from his knees and went into his room to study all that he could. When he got to school and began to take the test, he recognized that all the questions on the test were miraculously the same ones he had studied during the brief time he had the previous night. He passed the test, and he felt his faith getting stronger and that God knew him. Due to these life circumstances, he also began to develop a deep interest in helping the impoverished, marginalized, and disabled.

It was there at Government College University that Stephen met many new friends, including a friend who invited him to come to his brother's church to hear a sermon he would be preaching—a sermon that contained a warning about a book from America.

5

SHARING THE GOOD NEWS

I COME FROM A FAMILY OF TENNIS PLAYERS. MY GRANDPA SANK AND his brother Buck played in the US Open, my dad played for BYU, and my parents played in leagues with their friends at a tennis club near our house. My brother Scott was one of the best players in our high school, and I came to love the sport too. My family used to sit around the TV and watch players like Bjorn Borg, Chris Everett, and Jimmy Connors.

By 1984, when I was fourteen years old, John McEnroe had won six grand slam singles tennis titles—including winning Wimbledon in 1981 and 1983. After his first match of the 1984 Wimbledon tournament, he wouldn't allow cameras in "the interview room,"[4] saying he would "let his racket do the talking."[5] By the end of the tournament, he successfully defended his title by defeating Jimmy Connors 6–1, 6–1, and 6–2 in only eighty minutes and with only four unforced errors in the match.

One of the things I have learned from Stephen's early missionary efforts in Pakistan is to *let the Book of Mormon do the talking*. Notice

---

4. *London Times*, June 26, 1984, 32

5. *London Times*, June 26, 1984, 32.

how prophets of God describe the Book of Mormon (emphasis added in each):

- President Ezra Taft Benson: "Combined with the Spirit of the Lord, the Book of Mormon is the greatest single tool which God has given us to convert the world. If we are to have the harvest of souls that He expects, then we must use the *instrument* which God has [ordained] for that task—the Book of Mormon."[6]

- Elder D. Todd Christofferson: "The Book of Mormon is the tool—the *sickle*, if you will—that we are to thrust in with our might in that great field that 'is white already to harvest' (Doctrine and Covenants 12:3)."[7]

- Elder Gary E. Stevenson: "The Book of Mormon is the *engine* that powers conversion and a change of heart, leading us closer to Jesus Christ."[8]

- Elder Jeffrey R. Holland: "The Book of Mormon is the preeminent *net* God has prepared for missionaries to gather scattered Israel in these last days."[9]

- President Russell M. Nelson: "The Book of Mormon is a *gift* from God to all humankind."[10]

- Joseph Smith Jr.: "I told the brethren that the Book of Mormon was the most correct of any book on earth, and the *keystone* of our religion, and a man would get nearer to God by abiding by its precepts, than by any other book."[11]

---

6. Ezra Taft Benson, "A New Witness for Christ," *Ensign*, Nov. 1984, 7.

7. D. Todd Christofferson, quoted in Sarah Jane Weaver, "Leaders of the Church Teach from 'Preach My Gospel' During 2023 Mission Leadership Seminar," *Church News*, Sept. 26, 2023.

8. Gary E. Stevenson, "The Ongoing Restoration" (Brigham Young University devotional, Aug. 20, 2019), 4, speeches.byu.edu.

9. Jeffrey R. Holland, quoted in Sarah Jane Weaver, "Elder and Sister Holland Identify the Most Important Figure in the Book of Mormon," *Church News*, June 28, 2018.

10. Russell M. Nelson, "A Testimony of the Book of Mormon," *Ensign*, Nov. 1999, 71.

11. Joseph Smith, in *History of the Church*, 4:461.

CHAPTER 5: SHARING THE GOOD NEWS

Stephen seemed to innately understand that the Book of Mormon was the instrument, tool, sickle, net, engine, gift, and keystone God had chosen to gather scattered Israel in Pakistan. He had tasted the fruit of the tree of life, and like Lehi, he could not wait to share it with others (see 1 Nephi 8:10–12). However, he faced several serious dilemmas as he pondered where to begin:

1. In Pakistan, it is forbidden by law to share Christianity with those of the Muslim faith. He needed to be respectful of that law and make sure to share the gospel only with Christians, even if Muslims showed interest.
2. His Christian family and friends belonged to other churches, primarily the Catholic faith. He wanted to be sensitive to their beliefs and traditions while not shying away from sharing new truths.
3. He wanted to tell people about a church they had never heard of and about which there were no representatives in their country. How would they react?
4. Although he had copies of the Book of Mormon to share and a few books that explained the fundamental doctrines of the gospel, he was still a new learner with little experience answering the tough questions about our faith.
5. Finally, he knew that sharing his Christian faith in a predominantly Muslim country could lead to significant persecution.

Despite these concerns, Stephen felt a lot like the ancient prophet Jeremiah, who said, "But his word was in mine heart as a burning fire shut up in my bones, and I was weary with forbearing, and I could not stay" (Jeremiah 20:9) Stephen could not forbear or stay; he knew he had to open his mouth with his Christian family and friends.

Stephen had a wonderful place to start. He was part of a discussion group that met at his father's house. These men would gather, eat food, and talk about various topics—including their Christian faith. Stephen saw this as the perfect opportunity to introduce his new beliefs and share copies of the Book of Mormon with his friends. He also began to teach them from the *Gospel Principles* manual, and miracles began to follow.

Eventually, Stephen sent me a letter asking when the representatives of the Church would come. He told me there were thirty-two

25

families who "take keen interest in this church." I was astonished that there was even one person who was interested. When I heard there were thirty-two families wanting to learn more and there were still no representatives to teach and baptize them, I felt an urgency to reach these elect people. For the first time in my life, I began to understand what the term "scattered Israel" really meant. I was also starting to see that the Lord was doing something more magnificent in Pakistan than I imagined.

I wrote to Stephen and let him know that we were working on sending representatives. In addition, knowing that I had just left on my mission, Stephen also wanted to see if he and his brother Sabastian could come to Toronto, Canada, with me to be full-time missionaries. Based on the miracles that were happening through him, I replied that he was much more valuable to the Church right where he was!

As his faith grew, his desire to share the gospel increased. He wrote, "I remember brother the time, when you sent me a big box full with 'Book of Mormon' and you can't imagine my passion for sharing the gospel to other people. I distributed all the books among my family members, relatives and friends living in different cities."

Stephen had a tremendous passion for sharing the restored gospel. He reached out to family members and other Pakistani Christians and non-Muslims who could read and write English. Once, in the early 1990s, he decided to give a copy of the Book of Mormon to his maternal uncle Patrick Pervaiz, who lived on the desert farm of Stephen's maternal grandfather. This journey began in Faisalabad and led Stephen on a challenging 262-mile (422-kilometer), eight-hour bus ride to Rahim Yar Khan, followed by a blistering trek on camel through the historic and culturally rich desert that straddles the border of India and Pakistan named the Cholistan Desert. When Stephen arrived at the Christian village named Chak 116/1-L, his uncle was not on the farm. Stephen waited for two days at the house and finally decided to leave the Book of Mormon on his uncle's desk with a note and his testimony. He returned home by camel and bus to wait to hear from his uncle.

Sometime later, Patrick contacted Stephen and said that he wanted to know more about the book. Stephen shared what he knew, and in time, his uncle was converted. Deeply influenced by the Book of

Mormon, Patrick embarked on his own journey, traveling approximately 390 miles (627 kilometers) to Karachi, south of Rahim Yar Khan. His spiritual transformation led him to join the group in Karachi, where he eventually became a counselor in the first branch presidency there. Patrick, an educated mechanical engineer who attended Catholic schools in Multan, inspired many through his transformation from a Cholistan villager to a faithful leader in the Karachi Branch.

Another book went to a man Stephen called Dr. Saleem. Interestingly, Dr. Saleem already had a 1923 copy of the Book of Mormon that he received while traveling outside Pakistan. Dr. Saleem had been searching for the church that pertained to the book for many years. When Stephen started to preach about the Book of Mormon, Dr. Saleem recognized it immediately. He joined Stephen's gospel principles study group and was filled with joy to find the restored gospel. Dr. Saleem often offered one of the prayers during the meetings. Unfortunately, he died before he had the chance to be baptized, but later one of Dr. Saleem's grown sons and daughter-in-law joined the Church.

Stephen's father, Barkat Benedict, offered up his home for gatherings when Stephen was sharing the Book of Mormon with his friends and family. As a result, most of Stephen's brothers embraced the restored gospel and were baptized. His brothers Sabastian Javed and Samson Imran Raza later served as branch presidents, and his other brothers Shakil Simon and Sabir Victor also became strong members. Sabastian Javed was one of the first missionaries called from Pakistan and served in Malaysia, Sri Lanka, and Islamabad.

Years later, on February 15, 1993, Stephen wrote to me, "I have distributed around 400 Book of Mormons among the people in the different cities of Pakistan. Sometimes people refuse to listen to my preaching; sometimes they accept my teaching at once. I know this was God's plan for this part of the world."

Despite the difficulties and persecution he experienced, miracles began to happen. Stephen was a willing servant in God's hands, but ultimately it was the "instrument of the harvest" that started to gather Israel in that corner of the world.

6
RESOLVING CONCERNS IN TORONTO

IN ANOTHER CORNER OF THE WORLD, I WAS HAVING MY OWN EXPERIences learning about the power of the Book of Mormon to gather Israel. On my mission, while serving in Brampton, Ontario, I lived in a town house with five other missionaries across the street from the soon-to-be-dedicated Toronto temple. There was a lot of excitement among us missionaries because it was during the time of the temple open house. We were given the coveted assignment of working in the basement of the temple where tours conducted by Church authorities concluded. It was also our job to have the visitors fill out referral cards in case they wanted a copy of the Book of Mormon or a visit from local missionaries to answer their questions.

Our area was flooded with referrals since we worked in the neighborhoods around the temple. In fact, our workload became so great it was difficult at times to have a full preparation day. Most of the referrals were for people with casual or passing interest, but I will never forget arriving at the doorstep of a middle-aged man named Leonard.

He had attended the open house and filled out a card requesting that missionaries come by with a copy of the Book of Mormon. He was a Bible-loving traditional Christian on a quest to find the true church of Jesus Christ. He was willing to give any church the opportunity to share their beliefs in hopes that they would match up with what he had learned from his intensive study of the Bible.

Amazingly, among other things, Leonard shared with us that he had concluded from his studies that the gospel had been taken from the earth and that he was looking for a restored church. We were beyond excited to hear this and could not wait to tell him the good news. He also concluded that men and women had the potential to become like their Heavenly Father. We were used to antagonists criticizing us for this belief. This sounded too good to be true. The Lord had placed one of His noble and great ones in our path.

I visualized Leonard someday becoming a great priesthood leader. We discovered, however, that Leonard was moving to Australia for a year in the next few weeks. We would have to meet with him frequently to teach him the lessons.

After progressing through the lessons, we came up against a concern that became very troubling for Leonard. From his reading of the Bible, he decided that the true church of Jesus Christ should honor the Sabbath on Saturday. After all, that was the seventh day—the day that God rested.

"Why do you observe the Sabbath on the first day?" he asked. My companion, Elder Jeff Mitchell, and I tried to give the best answer we could. As I remember, we explained that it was not the day of the week that was important but how we observed the Sabbath. Leonard was not satisfied, so we told him we would study the question and ask for guidance.

During our companion study, we learned that many Christians began to worship on Sunday as a celebration of the Resurrection. Leonard responded by saying that that was a celebration of the Resurrection, not the Sabbath. We eventually realized we were not going to convince him on our own. It was then that we learned a critical lesson about how to help people resolve concerns. In fact, it turns out that convincing people is not our job at all.

The thought occurred to us missionaries to ask Leonard how he felt about his reading in the Book of Mormon. We were surprised to hear that he hadn't read much. He assured us that he would read, pray, and strive to find out through a witness of the Spirit if the book was true.

We asked him to consider what it would say about Joseph Smith if the Book of Mormon was the word of God. Leonard said Joseph would have to be a true prophet. A false prophet could not bring forth a true book of scripture.

We then asked him, "If Joseph was a true prophet, what would that mean about this being the restored gospel, and the Church being the true church you're looking for?"

He said, "If Joseph is a prophet, then this is the restored gospel."

We asked Leonard how that truth would impact the teachings of the Church. He recognized that he would be able to trust those teachings. So we all concluded that the main concern that needed to be resolved was whether the Book of Mormon was true and not the day of the week we observed the Sabbath. The Book of Mormon would be the evidence.

When we returned a few days later, we were thrilled to learn that Leonard had read a significant amount of the Book of Mormon and was convinced that it was true. We then asked how he was feeling about Joseph Smith and the Restoration. He saw the powerful connection and said he believed they were also true. He had found the restored church he was looking for! His concern about the Sabbath became secondary now that he had a testimony of primary truths. We were honored to be firsthand witnesses to why Joseph Smith called the Book of Mormon the "keystone of our religion."

Unfortunately, due to family opposition, he was not able to be baptized before he left for Australia. Our mission president told him he should not create a wedge in his marriage. Instead, he should honor his marriage relationship, and in time he could join the Church.

Leonard moved, and I have not seen or spoken to him since. I often wonder if he was ever baptized. Perhaps he's teaching gospel doctrine in a faraway ward or branch and telling his story about finding the truth in Brampton, Ontario.

I learned through this experience that people gaining a testimony of the Book of Mormon is the key to helping them resolve concerns. President Benson taught:

We are to use the Book of Mormon in handling objections to the Church. . . .

All objections, whether they be on abortion, plural marriage, seventh-day worship, etc., basically hinge on whether Joseph Smith and his successors were and are prophets of God receiving divine revelation. . . .

The only problem the objector has to resolve for himself is whether the Book of Mormon is true. For if the Book of Mormon is true, then Jesus is the Christ, Joseph Smith was his prophet, The Church of Jesus Christ of Latter-day Saints is true, and it is being led today by a prophet receiving revelation.

Our main task is to declare the gospel and do it effectively. We are not obligated to answer every objection. Every man eventually is backed up to the wall of faith, and there he must make his stand.[12]

Whether taking a bus for eight hours and riding a camel half a day to a ranch in the Cholistan Desert in Pakistan, or responding to a referral from a temple open house in Canada, Stephen and I were learning to trust the power of the Book of Mormon to do all the heavy lifting in missionary work.

---

12. Ezra Taft Benson, "The Book of Mormon Is the Word of God," *Ensign*, May 1975, 64–65.

7

SEEKING FOR THE CHURCH

FROM OUR LETTERS BACK AND FORTH WHILE I WAS SERVING MY MISsion in Toronto, Canada, it became clear to me that the Book of Mormon had spoken to Stephen, and he was deeply converted by the Spirit of the Lord. He was actively sharing the gospel among his friends and family and was beginning to gather a group of Saints. However, he wondered if he, his family, and his friends would ever be able to make physical contact with a member of the Church and be baptized.

As time went on, Stephen received a letter from Elder Merlin R. Lybbert from the Asia Area Presidency. In their correspondence, Stephen learned that Rick Smith and Robert Simmons, two expatriate members of the Church working in Islamabad, were holding church meetings with their families. These men were also sent a letter from the Area Presidency with information about Stephen and several other Pakistani people who were searching for the Church. Stephen wrote to the men:

> June 22, 1990
> US Embassy, Islamabad
> Pakistan

CHAPTER 7: SEEKING FOR THE CHURCH

Dear Sir:

I introduce myself STEPHEN ANJUM S/O BARKAT BENEDICT from Faisalabad, Pakistan. I am member of the Mormon Church. Since a year ago I was anxious to know the other member of the Church in Pakistan.

Recently, MERLIN R. LYBBERT, 2nd Counselor from office of the Asia Area Presidency 7 Castle road, Hong Kong has sent me list of the members of Mormon Church in Pakistan.

I am very happy to find all of you. Really, it has given me satisfactory and happiness. Now I can share my religious terms with you and other members. I would like to know personally about you and other member in Pakistan.

I want to meet personally each member so that I could gain more and more knowledge about the Church. I want to go ahead in this Holy Church. I will be glad if you can spare some time for me whenever I come to Islamabad. Please let me know your residence and telephone no. so that I can contact you easily. Pay my greeting and wishes to your family.

Sincerely,

Stephen Anjum

Upon receiving Stephen's letter, the branch president in Islamabad, President Rick Smith, wrote and let Stephen know how happy he was to receive his letter and to find out that there were other Church members in Pakistan. He said he wanted to learn more about Stephen and how he had joined the Church (from Stephen's letter, he assumed Stephen was a member). He shared with Stephen that the branch in Islamabad had been growing and now had five expatriate families attending church. He invited Stephen to travel down to Islamabad to join them for church services and let him know they held meetings on Fridays from 1:00 to 3:30 p.m.

After learning this information, Stephen made the long journey by bus to the capital city to meet them. In his own words, Stephen described what happened next:

The next Thursday (October of 1989), I traveled all night on bumpy roads to get to Islamabad. There was very tight security arrangements in the Diplomatic enclave. In spite of my best efforts to find the home of Bob Simmons, I failed due to a road block.

33

Disappointed, I returned back home and became very busy in my new bank job.

After a few weeks, I tried again, this time with my close friend Arif Boss. Again, we could not get past the heavy security. I tried a third time after several more weeks with two other friends, Saleem Javed and Marian Edmond, in hopes of finding the church people in Islamabad. But once again, we couldn't locate the home.

Later, I was invited by a Christian charity called the Focolare Movement to attend a meeting in Islamabad. I thought this would be another chance to find Bob Simmons" home. At the meeting, I met two new friends Razzaq Gill and Sikandar Bhatti. During the meeting I was sitting beside Razzaq, who was smiling and friendly. I told him that I was hungry and asked him if he wanted to go to a nearby restaurant and get some food. Razzaq smiled and said, "Let's go!" He took us to a very big and expensive restaurant. I was confused. I checked my wallet to see how much money I had in it. I found that I had only enough money left to buy a ticket to get back to my home. I told Razzaq that I could not afford the expensive food here, and that I did not want him to spend money on me. He gave me a big smile and asked me not to worry. After a few minutes, the food was on the table and Razzaq appeared dressed as a chef. I laughed out loud; he hadn't told me he was a chef at the restaurant! It was such a pleasant surprise, and we had a wonderful time together.

After the meal, I said, "Razzaq, I also want to give you a gift." I took out a Book of Mormon from my bag and gave it to him. He looked very happy, and I told him about the church and Bob Simmons. I gave him the address of Bob Simmons' home and asked him if he could find it by the next weekend, so that we could attend a sacrament meeting together. He said that he would.

I said goodbye to Razzaq and returned to the Christian meeting and gave a copy of the Book of Mormon to Sikandar Bhatti, who was very friendly with me. Before we departed, we promised to attend the church together. I told him, "This is the true church." I shared that I had many friends in Faisalabad and encouraged him to share the gospel with his own friends. I continued my missionary work by writing letters to my close friends and visiting many of my family members and friends.

Chapter 7: Seeking For the Church

The next Thursday, I made the eight-hour journey again and met Razzaq. This time, we successfully found the home of Bob Simmons. Finally, in November 1989, I met Bob at his house. This was the first time I was able to attend a sacrament meeting in Islamabad. I was given more church literature and felt greatly encouraged.

Meanwhile, Razzaq spread the good news among his circle in Sialkot, Daska, and Islamabad and I introduced the gospel to my cousin, Paul Anjum, who was working at the German Embassy. Paul later became a counselor in the Islamabad branch along with Razzaq. Both Razzaq and I, under the guidance of the Holy Spirit, began self-missionary work. We gave the contact address of Bob Simmons to others, and soon, people started visiting Bob Simmons out of their own interest, each with their own story of coming to know about the church.

The Lord began to pour out the Spirit upon Pakistan, and several pioneers from various cities in Pakistan began to emerge. Brother Simmons shared:

At first, I felt a bit protective and a little hesitant to open the gates when many investigators started coming to our home for Church, and on other days, to learn about the gospel. I didn't know their true intentions—there were so many from so many different cities of Pakistan. . . . In the year 1989, Pakistan was cited as having the most terrorist related incidents in the world. In 1988 the U.S. Ambassador and others had been killed, and a U.S. building had been attacked by a mob in the wake of the Salmon Rushdie affair. Moreover, Islamabad had been hit by numerous rockets, killing a number of people when suspected terrorists set off a large ammunition dump near the city. Additionally, we didn't even have permission to baptize any of these people, so I felt a little nervous letting all of these strangers in. Then I felt the Spirit whisper, "Just open the gates and let them in." . . .

One morning as I was sitting at the dining room table during gospel essentials class, I looked around me and realized that there were eleven men there, representing several cities from Pakistan. Virtually all of them were leaders in their respective communities. Three were preachers, another head of a Christian welfare organization, another the principal of a high school, the head of a transport

35

company, a schoolteacher, and a number of young men who had been involved as Christian youth leaders and boy scout leaders. I thought, how extraordinary. The Lord is certainly pouring out His Spirit upon these people and gathering His leaders, and among these sitting here are some of the future church leaders in Pakistan.

Stephen loved these meetings in Islamabad and most weeks traveled eight hours each way by bus on bumpy Pakistani roads to be part of them. Eventually, President Rick Smith returned to his home in Canada and Brother Niels L. Martin came and accepted the calling as branch president in Islamabad. On May 24, 1990, President Martin, who worked for the World Health Organization, went to Faisalabad with his security detail to meet with Stephen and his family and friends. President Martin reported in a letter to President Lybbert from the Area Presidency in Hong Kong what he experienced in Faisalabad:

> Stephen Anjum's extended family and the families of a number of friends are ready to join the Church. They refer to themselves as "members" and while I was there someone said that there are a number of "members" out in one village who want to be baptized. I asked how many there are who want to be baptized, and he said a total of about 100. . . . Limited to Faisalabad and the nearby villages there are no less than 50 who are very serious and who have testimonies.

Meanwhile, Stephen and I corresponded regularly throughout the two years I was in Canada. Stephen wrote to me about new developments, and I enjoyed sharing them with my fellow missionaries and friends in Canada. I continued to encourage him by mail. We began a close bond in those years.

By December 1990, authorization to perform baptisms in Pakistan had still not been granted. Many of the investigators not only desired baptism but were anxious that the Church be legally registered so they could perform marriages and have a graveyard to bury their dead. The Asia Area Presidency informed President Martin they would discuss these questions with the Quorum of the Twelve Apostles.

After a period of great unrest caused by the Gulf War, in which these investigators went into hiding and had limited contact with the

Church, tensions calmed in Pakistan. Accordingly, on March 20, 1991, the Asia Area Presidency wrote a letter to President Martin giving authorization to baptize worthy Pakistani Christians. However, out of respect for Pakistani law, they were not allowed to baptize Muslims.

Following this announcement, twenty people gathered for a sacrament meeting in Islamabad on Friday, April 12, 1991. Stephen and his close friend from Faisalabad, Marian Edmund, were among those in attendance. Plans were made for the first baptismal service to be held in Sialkot on April 18. The day was a remarkable success. Twenty-five Pakistanis were baptized into The Church of Jesus Christ of Latter-day Saints.

However, Stephen did not make it down for that baptismal service because he missed the bus to Sialkot. He was worried that he would be forgotten and that he had missed his opportunity.

Around that same time, my parents came to Toronto to pick me up at the conclusion of my mission. We traveled for three weeks to various Church and US history sites. Soon after we made it home, a letter arrived from Stephen. He wrote:

My dear Bro. Sean,

Greetings from Pakistan. You would be very glad to hear that I have been baptized on 10 May 91. Branch President Brother Niels L. Martin baptized me. . . . The church has been growing rapidly in almost all the cities of Pakistan. I hope by the grace of Holy Spirit, in near future many will get the baptism. The rate of membership in Church is amazing—28 members in 28 days.

Sean, I am very happy, I have received the Holy Spirit, and I am ordained as Aaronic Priest. I have received the gift of the Holy Ghost and being an Aaronic Priest I feel very happy. Although I am facing a lot of problems and criticism in my community, but I know that this church is true. I believe that the Joseph Smith is the true prophet of God. I believe that the Ezra Taft Benson is our present prophet. . . .

I have started working as missionary here in Pakistan. I have also received a video cassette and 10 Book of Mormon's sent by you. I gave all the 10 books to the people who were very curious about the Church and they have great love for the Church.

That mailbox in my front yard had just delivered another life-changing piece of news. I later found out that Robert Simmons and President Neils Martin decided they would come to him in Faisalabad to perform the baptism. I was thrilled to know that Stephen had finally received his first saving ordinances and was now a confirmed member of the Church. He had the gift of the Holy Ghost and held the priesthood of God. Stephen Anjum, a Pakistani man, was now a priest in the Aaronic Priesthood! I felt tremendous peace knowing that he and so many others had access to the fulness of the gospel. I felt humbled to have the opportunity to watch all this happen, even if I was all the way across the world. I was especially grateful to know that he had a connection with several inspiring leaders who could help him along the covenant path. My testimony deepened as I witnessed the Lord gathering His pioneers in Pakistan.

Enclosed in the letter were some pictures, one showing that first baptism in Sialkot and the other showing Stephen's baptismal service on May 10, 1991. (These pictures can be found at the end of this book.)

Robert Simmons recorded in his journal:

> President Martin interviewed him [Stephen Anjum]. We drove out to Rawal Lake and got here after a brief rain. We found a secluded spot and President Martin baptized him. . . . After the baptism I just felt good. We returned home and I confirmed Stephen a member of the Church. . . . [He received] a beautiful blessing in which he was promised that as he remained faithful, he would be an instrument in the hands of the Lord in bringing many, many people into the Church; he would be sealed in the temple; and he would teach the gospel in this land and in others.

Present in the photo of Stephen's baptism is his friend Razzaq Gill who had been baptized earlier in Sialkot. Razzaq was filled with a desire to share the gospel and was later called to serve in the England Birmingham Mission. He became the first full-time missionary from Pakistan to serve a foreign mission.

Several months later, on September 20, 1991, President Martin and Brother Simmons returned to Faisalabad upon Stephen's request to interview and baptize those he had taught. On that day, they held a sacrament meeting where about twenty-five people attended. President Martin and Brother Simmons spoke about Joseph Smith and the Restoration, the Book of Mormon, the plan of salvation, and other gospel principles, after which they held a question-and-answer period. They interviewed several young men. After a long day, by the light of a full moon, seven men were baptized in a canal passing through a park in Faisalabad. Stephen was then called and set apart as the group leader in Faisalabad.

In addition, on October 4, 1991, Stephen's brother Sabastian was baptized in Islamabad (since he had missed the baptism in Faisalabad). The gate of baptism had been opened in Pakistan. Full access to the covenant path was now available to Christian seekers. But that was just the beginning of the miracles about to occur in the life of Stephen Anjum.

8

THOMSENA

GROWING UP IN PROVO, UTAH, I HEARD OF SOME SPEEDY COURT-ships. But I had never heard of one that unfolded like Stephen Anjum's. When Stephen was twenty-six years old, his father, Barkat Benedict, proposed a traditional arranged marriage with a woman named Thomsena. Stephen was concerned with this idea because he had read about eternal temple marriage in the *Gospel Principles* manual. He wrote to me and asked what he should do. As a nineteen-year-old, I wasn't sure what to say! I did my best to teach him about the doctrine of eternal marriage and some of the Church policies surrounding that sacred doctrine. Stephen wisely went to counsel with President Martin, who advised him that it would be good to meet this woman and her family before he agreed to the marriage. According to typical Pakistani marriage custom, the bride and groom were not to meet each other until the wedding day. Regardless, Stephen made a trip to meet Thomsena.

When he arrived, Stephen knocked on the door of Thomsena's home and introduced himself. Her father was surprised to see Stephen at the door; this was not the way things were supposed to be done. Nevertheless, Stephen was invited in, and after meeting the family, he spoke with Thomsena's father—Yousaf Victor—about the marriage.

Yousaf was the headmaster of a Catholic school, and his family lived in a church compound in Rahim Yar Khan. He was a well-educated leader, author, and devout Catholic. He raised Thomsena to be a faithful Christian. During a time when women did not speak in church, Yousaf asked his daughter to do readings over the pulpit for the congregation.

Thomsena felt empowered by her father at an early age. At one point, Thomsena's love for her church was so strong that she decided to become a nun and entered the convent for training. However, just before she was to receive her habit (sacred religious clothing worn by nuns), her mother convinced her to leave the convent. Thomsena was their only daughter, and her mother hoped she would marry and have children instead.

As Stephen and Yousaf talked, Stephen nervously brought up that he was no longer Catholic and had joined a new church called The Church of Jesus Christ of Latter-day Saints. Stephen was worried about what Thomsena's father would say about having his only daughter marry a non-Catholic. Miraculously, Yousaf told Stephen that he would support him in his decisions. He approved the marriage with the condition that Stephen and Thomsena would marry in a customary Catholic ceremony. Stephen happily agreed. He was surprised by the love and respect he was shown. Clearly, the Spirit prepared the way by softening Yousaf's heart.

Customarily, the daughter would not have a say in the marriage arrangement. However, Thomsena's father approached her, told her about Stephen's new faith, and asked her how she felt about the marriage. Like her father, despite being a devout Catholic, Thomsena respected Stephen's beliefs and consented to the marriage. Stephen met her, and it did not take long for him to fall for her. She was beautiful and filled with confidence, charisma, and kindness. His emotions went from stress to peace.

Now that Stephen and Thomsena had met and knew they would be married, Stephen wanted to get to know her and build the romance. He asked Thomsena to walk with him in the gardens around the house. She agreed, and as they walked out the door, her mother yelled out that she wanted to come too!

As the three walked together, Thomsena's mother began to rub her beads and recite rosary prayers. She asked Stephen to join in reciting the rosary. He agreed, and the time was filled for half an hour with prayer. Stephen was not able to speak one word to Thomsena. He later said, "The romantic moment I hoped for was killed!"

Although willing to consent to the marriage, Thomsena's faithful mother acted as a diligent chaperone that day in the garden. Stephen and Thomsena would not see each other again until their wedding day.

Like Lehi and his sons after speaking with Ishmael, Stephen left their home ready to head into the wilderness as a Church pioneer in Pakistan with Thomsena by his side. Robert Simmons reported that when Stephen returned to Islamabad, his countenance was different. He was filled with joy!

On July 26, 1991, he and Thomsena were married. In a letter to President Martin following his wedding, Stephen wrote, "My wife is quite happy and all right. I shared my testimony with her; she took keen interest in the Church. My marriage programme was very excellent, beautiful, and cultural." Stephen later shared that on the last day of the wedding, a music night program was held at his home in Faisalabad. The program was organized by Stephen's new and old friends, with about 200 people in attendance. Razzaq, along with many of Stephen's other friends, entertained the audience by singing a cultural song. It was a fantastic evening of music, and both families (Thomsena's and Stephen's) sang and danced together.

Although Thomsena respected Stephen's beliefs and his new church, she was not interested in converting. The couple moved to Faisalabad, where Stephen was serving as the group leader of the church. Meetings were held in his father's home, and Thomsena faithfully prepared meals and helped Stephen host the many friends who attended. In addition to her other qualities, Thomsena is a skilled cook, and she often fed the church group delicious food such as chicken curry, chapati, and rice.

Thomsena reports she did this because of her love for her husband and not because her heart was turning toward the restored gospel. She continued to faithfully attend the Catholic church with some members of Stephen's family. Thomsena said she never felt the restored gospel "click" in her heart.

A humorous event occurred at church one day when a senior missionary couple visited. Couples were sent by the Church to provide member and leader support. Thomsena always focused on hosting and making things comfortable for everyone at church. When the missionary couple entered the house, they saw Thomsena busily preparing the sacrament table with a cloth and arranging the trays. The couple was surprised and politely informed her she needed to be ordained to the priesthood to prepare the sacrament. Thomsena naively said, "Okay, I'll make sure my husband gives it to me."

After realizing their innocent mistake, the Anjums apologized, and the kind couple told them they understood and provided the Anjums with proper training. Thomsena continued to help set up the room but left the sacrament to those ordained. Many years later, we all laughed together when they told us this story and reflected on how much they still had to learn in those early days.

Sometime later, Stephen wrote to me with exciting news. He said, "On 24th July 1992, God blessed me with a baby boy. I proposed his name as Sharon, this is the name of place where our Prophet Joseph Smith was born. I hope you will like this name." I, of course, loved his name! Amusingly, I later heard Stephen referring to his boy as Sharoon. When I asked him about it, he said he discovered Sharon was a feminine name, so he changed it to Sharoon.

A year and a half later, his second son, Reshayl, was added to their family on October 21, 1994. Both Sharoon and Reshayl (Ray) became the joy of their lives. These two boys were the first native-born members of the Church in Pakistan. Though quite different in personalities, Sharoon and Ray grew up supporting each other as members of a new church in a land where they were the minority.

As time continued, Thomsena felt a conflict with what she referred to as her double life. She read in the scriptures, "No man can serve two masters" (Matthew 6:24). She served those who came to her husband's church and simultaneously attended the Catholic church, praying with rosary beads and Hail Marys each night. It didn't feel right to her. As she and Stephen talked, Stephen invited her to read the Book of Mormon for herself and to pray and ask God if it was true. She agreed and began to read the book regularly.

Thomsena had been trained to become a teacher and understood the complexity of authoring a book like the Book of Mormon. She was astonished that a young man could produce something like that. She became convinced that Joseph Smith could not have done it without the help of God.

As she continued to read, she started to receive what she called the "clicking" in her heart. She felt the Spirit overcome her and knew that the Book of Mormon was true. Although she loved what she had learned from her Catholic faith, she came to know that The Church of Jesus Christ of Latter-day Saints was true. Elder Owen and Sister Pauline Morgan came to Faisalabad and taught her the six missionary lessons, and she was baptized on May 21, 1993, with two other converts.

When Elder Morgan asked her how she felt, she replied, "As I went down into the water, it felt like I was leaving behind my past life, and when I came up out of the water, I felt born again—a new person, ready to start a fresh and clean life."

Prior to Thomsena reading the Book of Mormon, the gospel did not "click" for her. When she opened the book and started reading, everything changed.

In the early years of their marriage, Stephen was also blessed with a good and stable job in the Standard Chartered Bank in Faisalabad. The bank job was demanding and required a lot of time in addition to his extensive missionary work and time leading the church group. Thomsena was a great support to him and helped him balance the load. As I'll talk more about in a later chapter, the Faisalabad group soon became a branch, and Stephen was set apart as the branch president. Stephen said:

> More and more people started attending church. There were lots of investigators and members were extremely poor. The branch had very little fast offerings to offer these people. I prayed to seek Heavenly Father's wisdom to solve this problem. I came up with an idea on how to best help these people who had strong faith, but economically they were very poor. Often, they did not have enough money to buy food to feed their families. After consulting

with my branch presidency, and some of my close friends, we came up with the idea to start a charity, so we could tap into the government resources, which were available for these poor people. On October 23, 1996, we formed a charity called "Tamir Welfare Organization." We registered it with the government of Punjab, Pakistan. In later years, we helped local communities with some mega projects, sponsored by the government of Pakistan.

Due to the significant work the Anjums were doing with the Tamir Welfare Organization, Thomsena was selected to become the district coordinator of "Bait-Ul-Maal" and "Punjab Bait-Ul-Maal" to provide funds for minorities and Christians. She ran a staff and became well-known in the community for this work. She led confidently and was sometimes criticized for being a female leader. Stephen was approached by others who were critical of his wife's actions. He proudly replied that he completely supported her. Thomsena said, "My father supported me and gave me the confidence to lead as a young girl, and my husband did the same for me as a woman."

Through their charity, the Anjums helped 4,000 poor Christian families get monthly pensions for five years. They also conducted different projects with British charities. Stephen traveled to Africa, South Asia, and Europe in the years that followed, representing the charity. In fact, his charitable work helped him fulfill one prophecy in his confirmation blessing stating that he would preach the gospel in many lands. He said, "My travels took me to Nepal, Bangladesh, India, Thailand, Kenya, Ethiopia, England, Italy, and France. Wherever I went, I shared my testimony of the Gospel. The Lord blessed me greatly for doing this."

On one occasion, while in Nepal, he met with a young convert who had been called as a branch president and was feeling overwhelmed and unqualified to do the work. Stephen told him about his own conversion story and the many miracles he had experienced. He said the Lord led the work and would use this young convert as His instrument.

The man was inspired by the conversation and said he now knew that he could do what the Lord had called him to do. Stephen left feeling happy to have been an instrument in the Lord's hands to help that young convert continue.

In addition to her work and leadership role in the charity organization, Thomsena served the Church in many capacities, including as Relief Society president. She and Stephen worked side by side sharing the gospel, building up the church they loved, doing work for the charity, and raising their boys. She is a woman of principle who leads with confidence and love, always serving her family and community.

9
MEETING M'SHELLE

ONE THING THAT STEPHEN AND I HAVE IN COMMON IS THAT WE both had an arranged marriage. Let me explain.

When I got home from my mission, I transferred to BYU. On my first day of school, I was standing in a line at the traffic office waiting to purchase a parking sticker. Standing two people ahead of me (and then due to some strategy, just one person ahead of me) was a beautiful girl with a bright smile, charming wit, and a shirt with blue polka dots. As I nervously began to talk to her, she immediately put me at ease with her kindness and outgoing nature. I played the role of an inexperienced new student and started to ask her questions about BYU. She was ready to answer and give me advice, and before we knew it, we were lost in conversation and a half hour had passed.

The parking counter was coming close. I knew immediately that I liked this girl, and I didn't want the conversation to end. As an awkward returned missionary, I couldn't muster the courage to ask for her number. Everything at the counter was speeding up and I saw my opportunity slipping away. I had figured out that her name was M'Shelle Lundquist but that's as far as I got. She went first to the counter then said goodbye and left out the door.

I hurried, paid, and went out the door hoping to see her. Relieved, I saw her over by her car lingering, but I hesitated and leaned down to tie my shoe while I thought of what I could say. When I looked up, she was driving away! No glass slipper was left behind.

When I got home that afternoon, my mom and I got to talking about my day and I told her about M'Shelle. When I told her I didn't know how to contact her, she gave me another great piece of advice like the day she told me to run down to Brother Millet's house.

She said, "What do you think BYU information is for?"

"What do you mean?" I asked.

She told me that since I had her first and last name, I could call BYU information and ask for her number.

"Really, you can do that?" I asked.

She assured me that was how it was done. What was there to lose? I called the number and gave them her name, and they gave me her number. It worked! Now I just needed the courage to call her. I turned off my brain and just did it. She answered and I somehow got her to say yes to a date a few days away up the canyon with my high school friends and their dates.

When I went to pick her up, she had forgotten my name, so she smartly sent her roommate to answer the door and ask my name while she waited around the corner listening. It was a great first date and I knew I wanted to get to know her more.

Before long, we were seeing each other regularly. On the last day of finals that semester, I drove her home, and we were talking in her car in front of her apartment. It was a chilly night, but our conversation was increasing in depth and eventually moved to a discussion about her plans. She had previously made an agreement with the Lord that she would need to know someone six months before she would decide to marry them. So she knew that if she did not meet somebody in her first week of school at BYU, she would be safe to turn in her mission papers. Little did she know that she would be meeting me on her first day of school!

In the car that night, she told me she wasn't sure what she wanted to do about her mission plans. I somehow (and to this day, I don't know what possessed me) blurted out that I thought we should get married. You could cut the silence in the car with a knife. M'Shelle looked at me in total shock and told me that she had thought that we were just starting to get serious and that it hadn't occurred to her to talk about marriage. I told her that I hadn't planned to say that—that it had just come out.

We drove up to the Provo Temple, parked, and continued our discussion. She told me she would have to think and pray about this, as it was the most crucial decision she would ever make in her life. I told her that I agreed and that I had no intention of rushing her into anything. Time passed for what seemed like an eternity, and at the end of the week, she called me and told me to meet her at her apartment because she had something she wanted to talk about.

I nervously drove to the Riviera apartments in my blue Subaru. My life was hanging in the balance. I knew that whatever it was that she had to say would completely alter the course of my life. She invited me into her apartment, and I cautiously sat down next to her on the couch. She told me that she had been praying and studying her scriptures and pondering whether it was right to marry me. Her study of the scriptures had taken her to Moroni 7. One night when she was reading, she stopped on verse thirteen: "But behold, that which is of God inviteth and enticeth to do good continually; wherefore, every thing which inviteth and enticeth to do good, and to love God, and to serve him, is inspired of God."

When she read those words, she felt the Spirit come over her, and she knew that getting married to me was God's will and that it would lead to good. Joy came over me like a flood, and I felt God's hand bringing us together. I was so relieved. Moroni 7:13 became my favorite scripture! There was the Book of Mormon again, significantly impacting my life.

After spending the Christmas holiday with her family, we got engaged in early January, and by the end of the school year, we were sealed in the Salt Lake Temple.

As we talked about our chance meeting that day in the parking office line, we realized that our schedules were completely opposite. When I was at school, she was at work, and vice versa. The only chance we had to meet was in that line on that day. Knowing what I know now about her, the life we have lived together, and the unlikely meeting in the traffic office, I would say our marriage was arranged by heaven.

From that point on, the long-distance friendship was not just between Stephen and me. It was now all about Stephen and Thomsena and Sean and M'Shelle. And then as kids started to come, it became all about the Anjums and the Dixons.

10

ESTABLISHING THE CHURCH

IN MAY OF 1992, THE SAME MONTH M'SHELLE AND I WERE MARRIED, Stephen was selected with four other members from Faisalabad to meet with Ed Davis of the Church's translation department to be considered to help translate the Book of Mormon into Urdu. Stephen was chosen to do the ecclesiastical review of the Book of Mormon. This required him to read other translations, give suggestions, and ensure accuracy. Stephen loved helping with the translation and, to this day, continues to aid the Church with translation projects.

In June of 1992, Elder Neal A. Maxwell and Elder Russell M. Nelson of the Quorum of the Twelve Apostles, along with Sister Maxwell and Sister Nelson, came to minister to the Saints in Pakistan. It was also announced that Elder John K. Carmack of the Seventy and President and Sister Jones of the Singapore mission would accompany them. Stephen made the journey to Islamabad to receive training from these servants of the Lord. At the suggestion of his aunt, he brought with him small statues of Christ with his name written on the bottom to give to the Apostles as a token of his gratitude. Stephen later saw President Nelson give a similar statue to Pope Francis and joked that it was the same one he gave!

The Pakistani *Millennial Star* (a local Church newsletter) for the month of September 1992 reported that:

> Elder Nelson spoke and commended the members for their faith in bringing the apostles and other visitors to Pakistan. He related that they had had flight difficulties along the way and at times were not certain if they would make it to Islamabad. The fact that they had arrived was a measure of the members' faith. He stated that nowhere else on the planet were there three General Authorities teaching the Gospel at that moment, making it a historic and significant moment.
>
> Stating that he was acting under the direction of Elder Maxwell, his senior in the Quorum of the Twelve, he then pronounced an apostolic blessing on the branch and the membership of the Church in Pakistan, as prompted by the Spirit. He said that this may be the only time in their lives the members present may hear such a blessing pronounced. He promised the members that if they followed the words of Christ and obeyed the law, they would be strengthened, they would prosper in their occupations, and they would be otherwise greatly blessed.

Following Elder Nelson, Elder Maxwell addressed the congregation. Again, according to the *Millennial Star*:

> Elder Maxwell was the final speaker and began his remarks by apologizing for how he looked. He said, "I must look like a sack of old doorknobs." He quoted Doctrine and Covenants 64:32—"But all things must come to pass in their time." He said that the Lord has His own timetable and that He had placed leaders in Pakistan at this time to further His work. He also quoted Alma 29:8, which states that the Lord grants unto all nations according to His wisdom. He had placed the Pakistanis in this place at this time, knowing long before they did that they would join His church. The expatriate members, whom the Lord has also placed here for leadership and nurturing roles, together with the Pakistani members will help the church grow in Pakistan.

Being in the presence of two Apostles had a tremendous impact on these new converts.

On February 2, 1994, Stephen Anjum was sustained as the president of the newly formed Faisalabad Branch. President Jones (the

CHAPTER 10: ESTABLISHING THE CHURCH

Singapore mission president), a member of the Asia Area Presidency, and a missionary couple from Hong Kong were in attendance. Marian Edmunds was sustained as Stephen's first counselor, and Salim Javed was chosen as his second counselor. The first branch meetings were held at the home of Stephen's father, Barkat Benedict. Stephen was grateful that his father was always supportive of the Church and was what Stephen referred to as a "dry Mormon" at the time of his death.

On April 15, 1995, with authorization from the Singapore mission president Carl D. Warren, a property was located to rent as a place to meet for the Faisalabad Saints. This property served as both a meetinghouse and a place of residence for senior welfare missionaries. Several missionary couples served there and greatly blessed the branch.

Stephen enthusiastically encouraged the members of his branch to serve full-time missions. While looking at the picture of the Faisalabad Branch on page 123, he and Thomsena identified nine branch members in the picture who served full-time missions, including his brother Sabastian. Stephen sent out many others while serving as branch president.

On October 11, 1995, an inspiring event occurred for the Saints in Pakistan. The Church received official recognition and a certificate of incorporation from the government of Pakistan. Just as six members were chosen in the state of New York when the Church was officially organized on April 6, 1830, seven pioneers, including Stephen Anjum, were designated to sign a document to grant official recognition for the Church in Pakistan. On page 119 and 120, you can find a picture depicting the front page of the certificate of incorporation and the names, occupations, and addresses of the seven signees.

Stephen was honored to be part of this group and to see the Church he loved obtain official recognition in Pakistan.

Stephen was also filled with a desire to take his family to the temple. He was constantly exploring ways to do so. On January 31, 1995, he wrote a letter to President Warren of the Singapore mission requesting information about how to attend the temple in Manila later that year. He had a month scheduled off work at the bank hoping it would work out, but the trip never materialized. On another occasion, he sought information on how to attend the temple in Switzerland.

53

The Anjum family and the branch at Faisalabad encountered a mountain of trials and opposition throughout the ensuing years. In fact, as the Church began to grow in Pakistan, it mirrored many of the struggles and trials faced by the infant church in New York, Ohio, and Missouri. During these trying times, Stephen never wavered in his testimony, although troubling circumstances in the branch kept him and his family away at times.

In an email written in February 2006, Luana Warner, who was a welfare missionary serving in the Faisalabad Branch during many of those years, wrote the following about Stephen's character:

> Sean, I think we knew the Anjums as well as anyone and we grew to love them. I judge them to be better persons than I am. I think the lives of hardship they have both lived have made it a necessity to live many principles that we in the United States talk about but do not really understand. Faith in the Lord Jesus Christ, pure love of family, patience and turning the other cheek are part and parcel of Stephen.
>
> Stephen had recently been released as branch president and his brother Sabastian was the new branch president when we came. We saw in Stephen dedication to the Gospel and sincere support and love for his brother. Besides coming each Sunday, Stephen came once a week and taught the youth seminary. This was a sacrifice of time and money. He did it without fanfare. He treated the half dozen students who came with respect and counseled them to prepare to go on missions. Stephen, more than anyone else in Faisalabad, had a vision of the future for those students and for the Church in Pakistan.

Stephen and I communicated through the ensuing years occasionally. It was always exciting and faith-inspiring to read his letters. Gratefully, the age of email arrived, which meant Stephen and I could communicate much more easily. Unfortunately, my computer broke and I lost his email address. Shortly after, the Twin Towers and the Pentagon were attacked in America on September 11, 2001. American welfare missionaries were immediately evacuated from Pakistan, and the Saints were left on their own during a challenging time. Christians were often seen as being aligned with Americans, and the members of the Church had to pass through great persecution and trials.

CHAPTER 10: ESTABLISHING THE CHURCH

Additionally, much time passed when Stephen and I were no longer in contact. I could not help but wonder how he was doing during so much turmoil. After a long while, I took a chance and wrote to an old address.

One day, when I arrived home from work, M'Shelle met me with a huge smile. She exclaimed, "You'll never believe who called you today!" She told me that Stephen had called and that she had spoken with him! He left a number to call him back. I had tried once several years before to talk with him on the phone, but the connection was so bad we could barely hear each other. I had given up on that possibility. That night, I called my friend in Pakistan and for the first time heard his voice clearly. It was a great blessing for both of us. We talked for about twenty minutes and vowed to remain in better contact. Afterward, we maintained regular email contact.

On June 5, 2004, Stephen wrote me an email describing some substantial changes in his life and an update about the growth of the Church.

> Greetings and love from Pakistan. Thank you very much for the letter dated April 24, 2004 which I received on 1 June 2004. Your letter gave me great joy and it reminds me the 15 years back time, when I wrote you about my first testimony. I am thankful to you for the Book of Mormon you donated to church and that book reached to me in the year 1988. That was the turning point of my life and Holy Spirit whisper in my heart that this is true book and Prophet Joseph Smith is true prophet of God. With the passage of time this belief become faith of my life. . . . Now more than 1500 people have joined the Church. In my hometown branch 80+ members attend sacrament meeting each Sunday. It is very encouraging to see our youth going on missions and serving the church.
>
> I got earlier retirement from the Bank service in the year 2000 and gave full-time to the charity. . . . In 1996, a small group of people of my friend established a Charity name "TAMIR Welfare Organization" registered with social welfare department (Government of Pakistan), committee choose me as President/Director of the Charity. LDS Charity supported TAMIR from the year 1999-2000 by sending us clothes, shoes, books, and medical supplies for the poor people of my country. We wish to re-establish

our contact with LDS Charity which we lost after 11 September 2001.

It is my vision that we are helping Jesus Christ in his mission on the earth. We are helping disabled people, vulnerable community, poor women and children, patients suffering with TB and AIDS. I have great love for the people and wish to help them through our charity. Heavenly Father heard our prayer and the Government of Pakistan and Community Fund U.K. are supporting our Educational and Health Programme. Me and my wife got Programme Manager's training from our neighbor country India in the year 2001 funded and supported by "Leonard Cheshire International" U.K. a leading organization in U.K. working for disabled people in 57 countries. In Pakistan we have a joint project called "Tamir-Cheshire Community Programme."

I love the Church of Jesus Christ of Latter-Day Saints and consider you my eternal friends and hope that someday I will be able to go to temple with my dear wife and children to have eternal marriage. We pray for the good health of your wife and new expecting baby. God bless you.

In only a few years, the infant church in Pakistan had grown from sacrament meetings with a few expatriate members of the Church to several branches filled with native Pakistanis and a visit from two Apostles, including the future president of the Church. The Lord miraculously hastens the work when the time is right. The time was right in Pakistan.

11

RAZZAQ GILL AND THREE COPIES OF THE BOOK OF MORMON

MANY OF STEPHEN'S EARLY FRIENDS WERE POWERFUL INSTRUMENTS used by the Lord to spread the good news of the gospel in Pakistan. Razzaq Gill, Stephen's friend who was the chef mentioned in chapter 7, was one of the most influential. He is a five-foot-tall spiritual giant!

Razzaq was one of the early Pakistani pioneers who immediately recognized the truth and then courageously devoted his life as a disciple of Jesus Christ. His personality and his love for Jesus Christ and the restored gospel fill every room he enters. His smile and laugh are unmistakable and consistently lead to the smiles of those around him. Razzaq's WhatsApp messages always come in three parts. First, he conveys his gratitude. Second, he communicates whatever information he wants to share. And third, he shares his testimony that the Church is true, Joseph Smith is a prophet, the Book of Mormon is true, and if we follow the teachings of Jesus Christ, we will have peace and happiness. He always ends by telling me to have a blessed life and a happy life and that God will bless me and my family and all the brothers and sisters.

He affectionately refers to me as "President" and M'Shelle as "Sister President." We can't get him to call us anything else. For

Razzaq, everything is about his love of God. I once asked him what he likes for breakfast, and he said in his endearing accent with a smile, "Whatever the God wants. God will provide."

Although quite different in personality, Stephen and Razzaq have a similar zeal for sharing the gospel. Stephen lived eight hours away from Razzaq in Faisalabad. His primary efforts in sharing the gospel and establishing the Church were in that region. Razzaq remained behind in Islamabad and focused his efforts there.

Living in Islamabad gave Razzaq the fortunate opportunity to be mentored and tutored by Robert Simmons, one of the great missionaries in the Church. When Robert opened his home to the various Pakistani people who were investigating the Church, he needed someone to help translate and teach all the people who were coming. He invited Razzaq to live in the helper's quarters along with his brother Mushtaq, who also became converted by reading the Book of Mormon. Razzaq was there at the unofficial headquarters of the Church in Pakistan to help Robert and the other expatriate leaders move the work forward.

Three Copies of the Book of Mormon

The contribution of expatriates like Niels Martin (World Health Organization), Doug Bradford (US Embassy), Rick Smith (Canadian Embassy), and Robert Simmons (US Embassy), among others, to move the work forward in Pakistan cannot be overstated. They were people of great capacity and faith. Together with their spouses, they made significant sacrifices to share the gospel and mentor those who were new in the Church.

Robert Simmons was driven by the invitation of President Benson to flood the earth with the Book of Mormon. Robert said:

> When we arrived in Islamabad, Pakistan, we had already taken up the invitation by President Benson to flood the earth with the Book of Mormon. We shared several with friends in Bangkok Thailand while serving there. One of them and his family joined the Church. We ordered many copies of the Book of Mormon to share in Pakistan, ultimately sharing a few hundred there.
>
> One thing I learned about flooding with the Book of Mormon was to not only flood to non-members, but with members as well. I

CHAPTER 11: RAZZAQ GILL AND THREE COPIES OF THE BOOK OF MORMON

would put 5–10 copies of the Book of Mormon on our dining table, telling the many investigators attending church in our home that they were free to take one, two, three or more copies of the book to share with family and friends, and then to invite them to church at our home. Many came. In this manner our branch and several other groups and branches of the Church were established as people came to our home to learn about the Church. We established branches in Islamabad, Faisalabad, Lahore, and Karachi, and church groups in Taxila, Rawalpindi, Gujranwala, and Sahowala.

One of the people we taught was Razzaq Gill (Stephen's friend). When the Gulf War came along, all our investigators stopped coming to our home, afraid of being associated with Americans. That is, all but one. Razzaq Gill. He continued to come to our home so I could teach him the gospel. He was among the first to join the Church. He also stayed in our servant's quarters along with his brother Mushtaq (we had two servant rooms) while he worked a job as a cook at a local hotel restaurant in the Islamabad vicinity.

One day Razzaq told me that he was going on a little vacation to his home in Sambrial, Pakistan, near Lahore. I put my testimony in three copies of the Book of Mormon and shared them with him, with the instructions, "Please share these copies of the Book of Mormon with three people who will become good members of the Church."

The Lord guided Razzaq, and the following happened with each book.

THE FIRST COPY

Razzaq shared one with Younis Shabaz, a Catholic schoolteacher in the Lahore area. When Younis read it, he knew that it was true. He came to the Simmons home to be taught the gospel. He arrived three days after the first senior missionary couple, Elder and Sister Hansen, arrived at their home. They taught Younis and he joined the Church. He moved to Taxila. Robert Simmons became his first home teacher and brought him translation materials from the Church translation department. He helped with the first translation of the Book of Mormon into Urdu.

59

The Second Copy

The second person Razzaq shared a copy of the Book of Mormon with passed the book along to his friend Patras Bukhari. The book sat on Patras's shelf for a year without him paying attention to it. One day, as he prepared for a long bus ride to another city to apply for a job as a teacher at a Catholic school, he went to his bookshelf looking for some reading material for the journey. He pulled down the Book of Mormon and decided he would try reading it.

During the journey, he fell in love with the Book of Mormon. When he arrived for his interview, the leader at the Catholic school had been called away and had made arrangements for Patras to stay and wait there for several days. From the Catholic school office, he looked up the number for The Church of Jesus Christ of Latter-day Saints and made a call that would change the course of his life. A senior missionary answered and invited Patras to come for a visit. Patras spent the next several days learning the restored gospel, and before he returned home, he was baptized as a new member of the Church. To say the least, that led to an interesting conversation with his wife when he got back home. He left to get a new job and instead came back as a member of a new church. The Lord prepared his wife's heart, and she joined him in his new religious journey.

Patras became a branch president only three months after his baptism, and he was the first native district president in Pakistan. He later helped with the translation of the Book of Mormon, the Doctrine and Covenants, and the Pearl of Great Price into Urdu. He eventually moved to America and received a PhD from BYU. He then returned to Pakistan and worked for the Church Educational System and is now employed by the Defense Language Institute in Monterey, California. He is currently working on the retranslation of the Book of Mormon and regularly provides the Urdu translation for general conference.

The Third copy

The third person Razzaq shared a book with was his old friend Peter Lawrence. After Peter was converted and baptized, he was called on a mission to Singapore. After serving there for several months, he was transferred to the Utah Ogden mission. This made Peter the first Pakistani to serve a full-time mission in the United States. As fate would have it, his trainer in Ogden was Gary Little, who is one of my close friends and colleagues in the Church Educational System. Following his mission, Peter stayed in Utah and joined the United States Army National Guard and became a tremendous resource due to his fluency in several Middle Eastern languages. His son also later joined the Army.

Thanks to the bold invitation from Robert Simmons and Razzaq Gill's willingness to share copies of the Book of Mormon, these three chosen men were converted to the restored gospel of Jesus Christ and were able to carry on the critical work of the Lord in their own unique way. Again and again, the Book of Mormon was central in helping the Pakistani people gain a witness of the restored gospel.

12

The Ways We Gather: Love, Share, Invite

Whether gathering Israel in Pakistan, like Stephen and Razzaq, or in Provo or Canada, the principles of effective gathering are the same. M'Shelle has taught me a lot about gathering Israel, which for her is never about consciously doing missionary work; it is always about loving the person she is with and bringing them into her circle. I have often looked over at the stranger sitting next to her on an airplane and heard them telling M'Shelle all about their life. She listens attentively, is authentic and real, and simply loves the person. Before they know it, they bear their soul to M'Shelle. She has maintained communication with a couple of these people for years.

I cannot count the number of times she has stopped a stranger to tell them they have the most genuine smile or the kindest eyes. They look at her surprised as if to say, "Do I know you?" You should see how she listens at church, as if she is hanging on every word and encouraging the speaker with her eyes.

One time when we were on an airplane with her two brothers and their wives, the flight attendant was going through all the usual information about oxygen masks, life vests, and what to do during an emergency.

Chapter 12: The Ways We Gather: Love, Share, Invite

Near the end, the attendant totally broke character, looked at M'Shelle, and said, "I'm sorry, but I have never had anyone listen to me like that before!" Her brothers never stopped teasing her about it.

On one occasion at a smoothie shop, she paid for the person coming behind her in line and left an uplifting quote with her name and number on it with the cashier. A few days later, the woman she helped texted her to thank her and they became wonderful friends. After meeting up and spending time together, M'Shelle involved the missionaries to help fill some of the needs the woman had—mostly friendship. Our family gatherings often have people M'Shelle has scooped up along the way.

However, my favorite M'Shelle "gathering Israel moment" was when she saw a woman in a lengthy line at Target with her two young girls at Christmas in California. M'Shelle and our daughter noticed the girls were watching a Christian cartoon on an iPad and were touched by this young mother's efforts. The woman ran to grab something she had forgotten, and M'Shelle offered to hold her place in line. After the woman checked out, M'Shelle told her about the Light the World campaign offered by our Church and wondered if she would be interested in joining in to do service for thirty days in thirty ways as a way to help keep Christ the focus during the busy holiday season. She gave her a card with the link that also had her name and number.

About twenty minutes later, the woman texted M'Shelle to thank her. She loved the idea and wanted more information. That friendship has now spanned six years. We had their family over for Thanksgiving and Easter, we attended their church, they attended ours, they came to visit us in Utah after we moved from California, and we returned to California for her daughter's quinceañera celebration.

M'Shelle's life is filled with meaningful friendships and opportunities to share the gospel because she simply loves people, and she is open to talking about her beliefs and traditions and allows others the same privilege. When it comes to sharing the Book of Mormon, I have found it is wise to consider the lessons I have learned from M'Shelle about loving first.

Let's be honest. For most people, the idea of sharing the Book of Mormon with a friend, neighbor, or stranger is terrifying. The natural man or woman within us says sharing the gospel with others might damage friendships or cause others to think we're weird. I don't blame you if you feel that way.

Additionally, the methods of sharing the gospel taught to you might not feel natural. Although our motives and love for the Book of Mormon may be strong, it is still challenging to get beyond the barrier of fear when speaking openly about our faith. In a worldwide broadcast held on June 26, 2021, Elder Dieter F. Uchtdorf, Elder David A. Bednar, Elder Quentin L. Cook, and Sister Bonnie Cordon discussed an inspiring approach to missionary work that emphasizes the idea of sharing the gospel in more authentic ways.

Based on this concept, the Church has launched an initiative to train members in sharing the gospel by focusing on three simple words: Love, Share, and Invite. Some of the previous methods advocated jumping right to the "invite" step, which felt forced or unnatural by some. But by emphasizing the need to love people and share our lives with them, many members feel liberated to share the gospel successfully. So let's look at what it means to "Love, Share, and Invite" and consider how this can help us flood the earth with the Book of Mormon.

LOVE

There is a common saying in real estate that when it comes to buying a property, it's about three things: location, location, location. Similarly, I think sharing the gospel is also about three things: relationships, relationships, relationships. When I say that, I don't mean relationships that lead to some end goal. In some sense, that's not a relationship. Rather, I mean true friendship based on love and concern for the individual.

One of the most common excuses for not sharing the gospel is not having any nonmember friends. The first step includes developing sincere relationships with people who are not of our faith. Genuine relationships thrive when individuals care about each other, serve one another, spend time together, and have common interests. Some relationships naturally become closer than others, but as you seek to get to know people and invest in your relationships with those at work and in the community, your opportunities to share the gospel in natural ways will significantly increase. As your relationships deepen, you will

CHAPTER 12: THE WAYS WE GATHER: LOVE, SHARE, INVITE

come to know what challenges your friends face in their lives. You will also likely come to know their feelings about their family, faith, and special interests, and they will naturally learn the same about you. As they learn what is happening in your life, and as they see your example, they may begin to ask you questions.

I was looking for a barber one day and noticed there was a shop in town run by a Hispanic woman. This was a terrific opportunity to improve my Spanish-speaking skills. So I went into the salon and was directed to a woman named Ruth who cut my hair. While she cut my hair, I spoke to her in her language, and naturally she wanted to know where I learned Spanish. I told her about my mission to Toronto, Canada, and how I had learned to speak there. She was fascinated by that experience. She asked me lots of questions and shared many of her own experiences while she worked on my hair.

I made sure to schedule my future haircuts with Ruth, and over time I learned her life story. She told me about the tragedy of her grown son who went missing in Mexico. When she shared that trial, she was understandably emotional. She also talked about the struggles of immigrating to the United States and raising a young son without a husband. Over time, our discussions turned to her faith, and we had meaningful conversations about the restored gospel, the Book of Mormon, and the Church. Ruth had heard about the Church in Mexico but didn't know much about it. She showed great interest in finding answers to her questions and developing a deeper relationship with the Savior. Ruth became a true friend, and my compassion for her and her situation grew.

Another opportunity I had to build an important friendship was with a young man named Casey who I met one day while he was stranded along the road. One early morning, I was pulling out of my neighborhood on my way to work when I saw Casey, a rough-looking man carrying a gas can and looking dejected on the side of the road. I felt prompted to drive over to him and ask him if he needed a ride to his car. He thanked me and said he had run out of gas and that the only gas station open that early was several miles away from where he had stalled. He had been walking for several hours.

In the car, he told me that he had, in desperation, offered his first prayer in years immediately before I pulled over. He knew that

God had answered his prayer. I asked him if he was a member of a church and he said he was not, but he was interested in learning more because he needed God in his life. Casey told me he was a recovering drug addict living in his car and was ready to change his life. He had grown up in our town and had many friends who were members of our Church who he respected.

We arrived at his car, and I was able to help him get it started. Before I left, I asked him if he wanted to join me and the missionaries for a lesson. He gladly agreed, and Casey and I began a deep friendship that would impact both our lives over the next several years.

Share

When you develop a meaningful friendship with someone, as I had with Ruth and Casey, it becomes natural to share your life with them. Friendships can start by talking about what you did over the weekend or a campout you went on with the youth in your congregation. Of course, in return, they will likely share about things in their life. Your sharing can come as conversations or include inviting them to one of your family events. One of my friends has a family mission statement: "Invite others to come and live life with us." I love the authenticity and simplicity of that. Come over to our house and play games, attend our children's events, and come on a double date with us. As we share our lives with others, they will see paintings in our home, observe family traditions, and see how the gospel impacts our lives.

Although my friendship with Ruth did not extend beyond the salon, we both felt free in natural ways to share our feelings about important subjects with each other. The situation with Casey was different. Casey was in such a bad way when I first met him that it was not safe yet to have him in the lives of my wife and children, but over time, as hope and light entered his life through repentance, his entire countenance and nature changed, and we invited him into our lives. We shared dinners, invited him for Christmas Eve, and had many miraculous experiences together. We were able to help him through the difficulties of his addiction recovery, and he eventually helped me improve my physical fitness when he became a CrossFit trainer.

Sharing comes naturally when you love someone and genuinely care about them. Discussing the Book of Mormon and the gospel of Jesus Christ with Ruth and Casey was not awkward. The Book of Mormon contains truths that they both desperately needed in their lives, and they were grateful. In fact, it would have been awkward *not* to share the Book of Mormon with them.

INVITE

When we think of inviting others to live the principles of the gospel, our minds typically go to a big invitation like "Will you listen to the missionaries?" or "Will you accept a copy of the Book of Mormon?" A friend constantly reminds me that we should invite people to do whatever is the next natural thing for them. For example, it could be coming to a neighborhood party, attending our child's baptism, or going out to dinner with us. When the time is right, and the Spirit prompts, invitations to accept a copy of the Book of Mormon or to meet with the missionaries will feel like the right next step.

One day as Ruth cut my hair, it was easy to ask her if she would like to meet with the missionaries. She happily agreed, and I sent the referral. Over time, she gained a witness of the truthfulness of the Book of Mormon and decided to be baptized. As I sat at her baptismal service, I started talking with another man who was sitting by me. When I asked him how he knew Ruth, the man told me she cut his hair. He said they had great conversations about the gospel and that he invited her to meet with the missionaries. I laughed and told him that I had done the very same thing! The Lord was the one who brought Ruth to the gospel. He just needed some people who would love, share, and invite.

I had the honor of baptizing and confirming Casey as a member of the Church. His journey was full of ups and downs, including a relapse following his baptism that led him to incarceration. Our friendship continued through his time in prison and his eventual release. Casey had the Book of Mormon and would read it tirelessly and send me pages of his deep understanding of the book and how it had helped him to come to know his Savior Jesus Christ. He told M'Shelle once that it had saved his life in prison. He kept his head down, stayed out of trouble, and read like crazy. When he got out, the Lord was able to transform his life.

Casey obtained meaningful employment, married a woman who loved him, and started working with troubled teens in an addiction recovery center. Tragically, he was later killed in a car accident. I was a pallbearer at his funeral. I love my friend Casey, and I am so grateful that the gospel of Jesus Christ brought us together. The opportunity for our family to love Casey, to share our lives with him, and to invite him to make changes led to many miracles that we cherish.

Gathering Israel in Provo or in Pakistan begins one relationship at a time.

13

LONDON, ENGLAND

AFTER SEVENTEEN YEARS OF STEPHEN'S CHURCH AND COMMUNITY leadership, the promise in his confirmation that he would be sealed in the temple still had not been fulfilled. The adversary was determined to thwart every effort the Anjums made to receive their saving ordinances in the temple.

In the summer of 2005, Stephen wrote me a respectful letter wondering if there was any way that my family could sponsor his family to come to Utah to be sealed in the Salt Lake Temple and to attend general conference.

My wife and our young family (which consisted of five children) went to a family party with my parents, siblings, and their families. I read Stephen's email and asked, "What should I say to him?"

Without hesitation, they said, "Tell him yes! We don't know how, but we'll figure it out."

I immediately wrote back to Stephen telling him that we would pay for the flights and that he could stay with us when he got to Utah. That was the easy part. What I didn't know was that the hardest part was getting a visa for the Anjums to travel to the United States.

Unfortunately, after considerable effort, their visa application was rejected. This was very disappointing news for all of us. However, I was impressed with Stephen's response. He handled it with grace and trusted the will of our Heavenly Father. I wrote to him that he should not give up on his quest to go to the temple and that he should explore opportunities in other parts of the world.

Later, as part of his work, Stephen was given the opportunity to fly to the Leonard Cheshire Charity headquarters in London. He saw this as a good chance to investigate whether his family could be sealed in the temple in London. He made an appointment to meet with the temple president, Rowland Elvidge. While traveling by rail to the temple from Norwich, he was presented with another difficult setback. His luggage, which contained his clothes, temple recommend, important documents, and other personal items, was stolen. He felt all alone and didn't know how he could proceed. He reported the incident to the Liverpool Railway Police and called the temple president. President Elvidge lovingly reassured him not to worry and that he could stay at the temple accommodation center while he worked things out. When he arrived, he was greeted warmly and was encouraged to bring his family back to London to be sealed. The temple workers would help him arrange all the details.

His roller coaster of emotions dipped again during his three-day visit to London when he received the heartbreaking news from Pakistan that his father had passed away. Stephen said, "Though I was filled with sadness, I looked toward the temple and prayed in my heart, hoping that one day I would return to perform the sacred ordinance of baptism for the dead on his behalf."

On September 7, 2005, He wrote me the following letter:

In the U.K., I had a chance to visit London Temple and had very good meeting with the President [Rowland Elvidge], who said that they can send me invitation letters and will do other arrangements etc. There is very nice proper arrangement of accommodation as well as temple clothing. I am very excited for temple blessing as well as baptism for the dead. I have plan to go in the month of December 2005. I shall write you soon about everything. I don't know your offer to support my family for temple visit is still exist or not. My family still needs your support for visiting temple and it is easy for my family to get U.K. visa. The British High Commissioner Mark Lyall Grant knows me, and my family very well and my recent visit to U.K. was sponsored by British High Commissioner. I shall soon write you in detail.

Your brother,

Stephen Anjum

Stephen's hope to bring his family to London in a few months meant we would all have to work quickly. My family started fundraising, and we approached my wife's family, the Lundquists. Our parents and siblings on both sides made great sacrifices to help with the money needed. They gave generously without hesitation. We also received a check from a friend that provided the final amount we needed. We booked a flight for the Anjums from Pakistan to London for December 4 through 11. In addition, letters had to be sent to the British Embassy in Islamabad from the temple and from me explaining the nature of the trip, confirming accommodations at the temple, and providing proof of a return flight.

Soon thereafter I received a phone call from my mom. She said, "Sean, how would you like to go to London to escort the Anjums through the temple?"

"Yeah right, Mom. It took all we had to get them there," I replied.

"I figured out that I have just enough frequent flier miles to send you."

This sounded too good to be true! I called M'Shelle and she was thrilled for me.

That Sunday I bore my testimony in the ward where I was serving as bishop and told them of this wonderful opportunity to go to London to escort my Pakistani friends through the temple. By the time the meeting ended and I had walked off the stand, I was approached by a close friend. He told me several people had just spoken with him at the end of the meeting and wanted to inform me that M'Shelle was going with me. He referred to them as "the others" and said they would pool their efforts to take care of her flight.

We felt humbled by their generosity and this act of friendship. I was happy to know that M'Shelle and I would get to do this together. It would not have felt complete without her.

Two days before we were to fly out, we received a very discouraging email from Stephen. He informed me that the holiday rush in the embassy meant they would not be able to interview Thomsena for her visa until December 12—one day after they were to return from London. Nothing could be done to move the date up, and our tickets had to be canceled and the trip postponed.

We could feel the power of the adversary trying to thwart the Anjums' efforts. To be honest, M'Shelle and I felt quite deflated. It seemed like this chance to meet the Anjums and to witness them receiving the crowning temple ordinances was too good to be true. However, we knew that we had to persevere against all obstacles. I immediately wrote an email to Stephen knowing that if we felt deflated, he must feel much worse. In the email, I wrote:

Dear Stephen,

I guess we shouldn't be surprised that we are facing opposition and obstacles while preparing for such a sacred event. This is just a sign that truth is at work. We just need patience while we wait a little longer for our great reunion. We know that God is in charge and that we must submit to His will. While I was serving my full-time mission in Canada my mom sent me a quote that said, "Don't pray that your trials will be removed but that you will have a strong enough back to bear them." We have waited for 17 years. I guess we can wait a little longer. We know that you did all in your power to make this work on schedule. I think with the holiday season we got caught in a busy time for the embassy. We will be praying for Thomsena on the 12th!

Fortunately, on December 12, Thomsena passed her interview and we were able to reschedule the tickets for January 31 through February 8, 2006. We eagerly began preparing for our trip, knowing that their visas were in hand and the tickets were purchased. We felt a burst of energy. We began to collect a bag full of gifts that we thought would be a blessing to the Anjums and their branch in Faisalabad. We went to the distribution center and purchased several DVDs and other items we thought they would enjoy. We also went to the dollar store and purchased various American toys and candy. Our three oldest children, Lisie, Jared, and Robby, donated their hard-earned money to help in this effort. Members of our ward donated other items.

In addition, our family piled into the van and drove to several sites that we thought the Anjums would love to see on video. We filmed BYU, the Provo Missionary Training Center, the Provo Temple grounds, and several chapels along the way. We then went to Salt Lake City and filmed Temple Square and the Conference Center. We thought this would be one way the Anjums could fulfill their dream of seeing Church headquarters.

The day had come for M'Shelle and I to begin our journey to London. After landing at the London Gatwick Airport, we took a cab and traveled through the English countryside to the temple accommodation center. We drove through the iron gates and along the pristine grounds of the temple. We were soon met by Elder Henry Florence, one of the temple missionaries. He became a dear friend and was immediately drawn in by our purpose for coming to London. Elder Florence was determined to do everything he could to make this occasion comfortable and meaningful for the Anjums.

Knowing that the Anjums would not be arriving for a couple of days, we took a quick trip to France to visit the sites in Paris. Elder Florence told us he would welcome the Anjums and get them settled, realizing we would be returning shortly after they arrived.

Although Paris was captivating, we couldn't wait to get back to England to meet our friends. We expected that the Anjums would arrive about an hour before our return.

Before our departure, Stephen told me by email that Satan was doing everything in his power to stop the trip but that I shouldn't worry. He was never specific, so I trusted in the Lord and prayed for a miracle.

I had a troubling feeling come over me as we traveled back to the temple. What if the Anjums weren't able to get out of Pakistan and make the journey? M'Shelle and I became genuinely concerned about what we would find when we got back.

We put our things away in our room and I immediately knocked on the Florences' door. He greeted me with a smile and said, "They're here!"

MEETING FOR THE FIRST TIME

He told us they were a wonderful family and that they had arrived only twenty minutes before us. He said, "Come along, I want to introduce you." My heart began to pound as we went down two flights of stairs to their room. Their room was situated next to a lobby, and

73

we waited there while Elder Florence knocked on the door. I heard Thomsena's voice, and he invited them to come out and see a surprise.

Thomsena and her twelve-year-old son, Sharoon, came out first. She let out a happy scream and we hugged each other. She then gave M'Shelle a big hug. She was beautiful, kind, and full of warmth and love. Her son was handsome and mature beyond his years. We spoke for a moment and then Stephen emerged from the room. We moved quickly to each other and embraced for some time. There were tears and emotions that did not require words. He whispered the words, "My brother."

We were now united after a seventeen-year journey. The Book of Mormon became the instrument God chose to bring this family to the waters of baptism, priesthood ordinations, church leadership, phenomenal missionary success, and now to the doors of the temple. Stephen's playful eleven-year-old son, Reshayl, soon came out and we were introduced. As Stephen and I continued our reunion, our wives looked on and we instantly knew that our families would share a bond throughout eternity.

Stephen was everything people had described him as. He was humble and kind, yet I sensed great strength and power within him. It was easy to see why he had become such an effective tool in the hands of the Lord. Elder Florence had arranged to take our two families out to dinner. We went to a nearby restaurant and talked. There was so much to discuss that it was almost overwhelming. It was there, with beads of sweat running down his forehead, that Stephen told us just how close they had come to not being able to leave Pakistan.

He said that the day following Thomsena's successful interview, he became sick and was hospitalized for several days. He was diagnosed with diabetes in addition to his heart problem. The sponsors of his charity then requested him to go to India for an important meeting. The meeting would be held during his scheduled trip to London. He explained he could not, and they reluctantly let him arrive immediately following his trip to England. However, he needed to apply for a visa for the India trip. He did so and became incredibly stressed as his London trip approached and they still had not returned his passport. He took a bus ride to Islamabad on January 28 to get his passport back, and they told him they could not give it back until February 4.

CHAPTER 13: LONDON, ENGLAND

He told them he needed it for his trip to England on January 31. They said there would be no way to find it in the system until then.

He returned home dejected. The next day, he took the four-hour bus ride back to Islamabad. Again, he was unsuccessful. Finally, he told Thomsena to take the boys and meet him at the airport and the Lord would provide him with the passport. All the while, we were in Europe without any knowledge of this last-minute trial. Later that afternoon, the passport was returned. Stephen went to the airport, met his family, and boarded the plane. As he sat with us at dinner the night of the thirty-first, he informed us that he had not been to bed since the twenty-ninth!

Following dinner, we returned to the housing center and shared our bag of gifts with the Anjums. They were excited and grateful. Sharoon, Reshayl, and I enjoyed throwing a Nerf football around the lobby. They had never seen a ball like that. Much to our surprise, the Anjums had brought gifts for us. With a smile on her face, Thomsena gave a gift-wrapped package to my wife.

M'Shelle opened the package and found a beautiful Pakistani gown that had been hand-beaded by disabled people working in the Anjums' charity. She was also given traditional arm bangles. She was touched by this gift, especially as she pictured the many hours that these loving Pakistani workers spent just for her. I don't think any of us could wipe the smiles off our faces that night! Spending that evening together was incredible, but with the sacred ordinances of the temple awaiting us in the morning, we said our farewells.

Early that next day, we walked across the temple grounds with the Anjums to the door of the temple. We were met by Elder Florence and his warm smile at the recommend desk. We showed him our recommends and then went into the lobby. To our surprise, another obstacle presented itself. When giving the Anjums their temple recommends, the district president had only provided the standard temple recommend and not the recommend to perform live ordinances.

President Elvidge was made aware, and a secretary in the temple was put to work trying to track down their priesthood leader in Singapore. After about an hour of waiting and paperwork, he was located, and permission was granted to proceed. President and Sister Elvidge took a personal interest in the Anjums, walked us through the temple, and trained and prepared them for the ordinances of the day. They were warm, inspiring people who really put a special touch on the experience. They and the other temple workers treated Stephen, Thomsena, and their boys like royalty while they were in the temple. I went with Stephen as his escort and M'Shelle went with Thomsena.

Following the initiatory ordinance, Stephen was personally taught by the first counselor in the temple presidency in a private room. M'Shelle said that Thomsena and she had a similar experience with the temple matron, Sister Elvidge, who took Thomsena into the special bride's room and invited her to select a dress of her choice from a beautiful collection.

I will simply say that being by the side of my friend as he received his endowment was one of the greatest experiences of my life. Both he and Thomsena were focused and attentive. It was evident they were taking this covenant experience seriously. They soaked in every bit of information that they could. President and Sister Elvidge had rightly explained that they should just enjoy the experience and not worry about getting everything down. They were told that the Spirit would be their teacher while in the temple.

After the endowment ceremony, we spent a moment with the Anjums in the celestial room. We soon moved to a beautiful sealing room. The room was filled with senior missionaries and other interested temple workers. I was asked to be a witness. The Spirit was present as the Anjums knelt across the altar from each other and were told to look into the mirrors representing eternity. The ordinance was performed.

My thoughts centered on the majesty and power of God in making this all possible. Eventually, the sealing room doors were opened, and Sharoon and Reshayl entered dressed in white. They truly looked like angels sent from heaven. They joined their parents around the altar and were united as an eternal family. Words cannot adequately describe the moment. Stephen and Thomsena had now received all ordinances necessary for them to be exalted in the kingdom of God. Now their task as a family is to keep those sacred covenants and watch the grace of Christ operate in their lives.

The next morning, we were excited because we could all go into the temple to do baptisms for the dead. As an Aaronic Priesthood holder, Sharoon could participate in the baptisms and confirmations. I distinctly remember standing in the font with Stephen as I prepared to baptize him for the dead. I thought of a letter Stephen had sent me back in 1990 where he said that his greatest wish "was to be baptized by [my] hand." I reminded him of this letter, and we smiled at what was now taking place.

I baptized him and his son. He in turn baptized me and his wife several times. The feeling I had was a mixture of intense spirituality and pure joy. It felt good to do the work of the kingdom alongside my brother in Christ.

M'Shelle spent the day with the temple secretary, Maurine Butcher, copying important documents Stephen had brought with him from Pakistan. She put these documents in sheet protectors and binders so that they could be preserved. Many of these letters and documents served as my sources for the writing of this story. They answered many questions we had and introduced many new plots and subplots to the story.

That evening we were invited to present a fireside with the Anjums in the temple visitors' center. Approximately sixty interested temple workers and ward members attended. The Spirit was strong as we testified of the power of the Book of Mormon to help gather Israel and shared the miraculous story of the Anjums' conversion. In addition to sharing their testimonies, the night was concluded with Stephen, Thomsena, and their boys singing "I Am a Child of God." There were few dry eyes in the building. It was a perfect ending to a beautiful night.

On Saturday, the Anjums traveled to London to spend some time with Pakistani friends who had moved there. M'Shelle and I did some more sightseeing and attended the theater, and then we met together late that night to say our farewells. I gave Stephen a piece of the Salt Lake Temple with an engraved plaque stating that it had been removed during renovation. He was pleased to have such a rare treasure. My hope was that it would remind him of his sacred covenants and our cherished friendship.

The next morning, before M'Shelle and I left to return home, Thomsena awoke early to prepare some authentic Pakistani food for us. We all embraced and said our goodbyes, not knowing if we would ever see each other again in this life.

14

A New Life in England

Shortly after we arrived home from England, we received an email from Louise Lucilla, the London temple secretary. She wrote:

> It was a blessing for all of us to meet you and the Anjums. Those boys are so bright and cute. The whole experience is something that we will all remember for quite some time. The Sunday you left was Fast and Testimony and Brother Anjum bore a wonderfully touching and profound testimony. I am just so impressed by the way our Father has brought together two nations of such vast cultural and religious differences and made them as one. By such simple means. I know I should not be amazed, but I am. Thank you for bringing that experience to us.
>
> Best Regards.
> Louise Lucilla

On Saturday afternoon, February 11, my son Jared came running into the room saying that Stephen Anjum was on the phone. He was checking in to see that we made it home all right and to let us know of the spiritual outpouring that had occurred when he got home. He said his family and friends from the branch wanted to hear all about their experience. Stephen said many who were not coming to church expressed a desire to come back. He shared deep gratitude for the whole experience.

After the phone call, we exchanged emails. The following is an excerpt from an email I received from him.

> On the 9th Feb 2006 morning we were at the Islamabad, where my brother Samson and two colleagues received us at the Islamabad airport. On Sunday, 12 Feb 06, 14 family members attended sacrament meeting and I shared my Temple experience and testimony in the Sacrament Meeting and on Sunday, 19 Feb 06, I showed the Utah Tour video in the Sunday School meeting. Everyone in the branch was very happy to listen to our beautiful experience of temple visit.

Stephen and Thomsena rejoiced that they had received their temple endowments and were sealed together as an eternal family. Bringing that unique experience back to the branch and their extended family provided a new strength for everyone.

As the years passed, Stephen and Thomsena continued to serve in the Faisalabad Branch and labored hard to champion the rights and needs of both women and the disabled through their work with the Leonard Cheshire Charity. Their work and faith in Jesus Christ brought them tremendous joy, but it also brought unimaginable challenges and persecution.

A whole other book could be written about the hardship and difficulty the Anjums have endured throughout their lives. Driven by the need for safety and stability, the Anjum family relocated from Pakistan to Birmingham, England. Leaving behind their homeland where they were making such a significant impact on both the Church and their community was a trial that took a major toll on their family.

In England, they were refugees with limitations on their ability to work and earn a living. They went from being the ones serving to being the ones needing to be served. They experienced financial, physical, cultural, and emotional hardships of every kind. Thomsena described her experience in this way:

> We came to England to keep our family safe. Life changed so quickly that there was no time for us to accept our new reality. We were self-sufficient people in Pakistan. We had seen hardships, but

the Lord had blessed us greatly. Where we once helped the needy, we found ourselves in need in the UK. We had to wait for money from the government and wear clothes that people gave us. And then, a new kind of fear developed: the fear of being sent back.

This is to share that we started from nothing and built a beautiful home in Pakistan, only to leave and restart the process with our hands tied. Many times, my son wouldn't have enough for lunch at school. But trusting the Lord meant He would always find a way for us. Sometimes it was food from church members, sometimes the stipends came just in time, or at times we'd even find literal cash notes lying in the street, seemingly placed by the hand of the Lord. We never went to bed hungry. In times of great need, God showed us the way or touched someone's heart to help when we least expected it. Our Church was our anchor in this sea of change.

I always hold close to a particular scripture from Doctrine and Covenants 122:8, which speaks of how Christ condescended for all, for our sake. This scripture constantly reminds me that He is acquainted with all our pains and struggles. This challenging time brought me closer to Him. Since then, I have prayed and read the scriptures every morning. Another blessing was being able to visit the Lord's temple; this change brought me peace and a clearer perspective. I'm grateful for the temple being near us, for the restored gospel, and for the Prophet Joseph's translation of the Book of Mormon.

Now the Book of Mormon was not just a missionary tool they could share with others as the evidence of the Restoration, but it continued to be the means of drawing them close to their Savior Jesus Christ so that they could have the faith to endure the various trials of their lives. Despite the difficult circumstances, the Savior has been with them every step of the way, manifesting His tender mercies just as was promised in 1 Nephi 1:20: "But behold, I, Nephi, will show unto you that the tender mercies of the Lord are over all those whom he hath chosen, because of their faith, to make them mighty even unto the power of deliverance."

The Anjum boys went through high school in England and became acclimated to British culture and made friends. Their second son, Ray, has a keen sense of humor, a knack for storytelling, and a talent for filmmaking and photography. The family made various sacrifices in those years so that he could pursue his dreams. He worked hard and eventually earned a bachelor's and master's degree in cinematography.

Their elder son, Sharoon, felt the weight of helping his parents support the family during those difficult years of transition. He always wanted to serve a full-time mission for the Church, but various obstacles kept making that goal seem impossible. Sharoon wrote of this time:

> My family and I arrived in the UK as asylum seekers, fleeing religious persecution in Pakistan. We faced repeated court rejections, and each day was fraught with the looming dread of deportation. The Home Office finally accepted our case after five arduous years. The shattering of the glass ceiling liberated us from the limbo of uncertainty, marking the onset of a new life. However, we had yet another summit to conquer. Seeing my family's struggle, I, as the eldest, assumed responsibility. As a refugee, barred from pursuing higher education, I juggled minimal jobs to support my family, especially after my father underwent a quadruple heart bypass surgery. Despite these challenges, I persevered and remained resolute in my commitment to create a better life for us. Eleven years after our arrival, I experienced a powerful urge to serve the Lord.

Despite Sharoon's desire to serve a mission, he thought he had missed the opportunity and would need to move forward with his life. However, the thought of serving persisted in his mind. At age twenty-five, Sharoon submitted his papers and awaited a mission call. He then posted this on Facebook:

> Dear Elder Anjum,
>
> You are hereby called to serve as a missionary for the Church of Jesus Christ of Latter-day Saints. You are assigned to labor in the England London Mission. It is anticipated that you will serve for a period of 24 months . . .
>
> Thank you all for your support, I hope I can be an instrument in His hands. I just want to share Jesus is the Christ, Savior of our world and when I read and listen to His words, I feel his love.

Sharoon's call brought joy to so many of his friends and family who knew of his desire to serve. His courage and faith compelled him to press forward with steadfastness in Christ in the face of many obstacles. Sharoon began his missionary service on the streets of England, the same country where, more than a quarter century before, some other Latter-day Saint missionaries gave a copy of the Book of Mormon to a Pakistani pastor in Bristol.

15

LET THE BOOK SPEAK FOR ITSELF

ONE OF THE REASONS WHY THE GOSPEL STARTED TO SPREAD IN Pakistan was early members and the expatriate Church leaders trusted the Book of Mormon and allowed it to speak for itself.

My daughter Lisie, who is the same age as Ray and a year younger than Sharoon, also learned this important lesson while serving as a missionary in the Tennessee Nashville Mission. She was working with a man named Larry who had been involved in his evangelical congregation in Fulton, Kentucky. In her words, here is what happened:

> My brand-new companion and I had just been transferred to Fulton, Kentucky where we were replacing a set of Elders, so we didn't know the area or anyone in our new church congregation.
>
> On our first Sunday on my way out of sacrament meeting a hand caught my shoulder and turned me around. I was greeted by a warm southern woman with a great big smile and cowboy boots. She introduced herself as Roberta Moorehead and almost in the same breath told us that she wanted us to come by and teach her husband Larry who wasn't a member of the Church. As missionaries with nobody to teach yet we were thrilled.
>
> However, our excitement was soon shadowed by a warning from another member that Larry was known to be hard on the missionaries and the doctrine of the Church and that he had been

84

CHAPTER 15: LET THE BOOK SPEAK FOR ITSELF

a Pentecostal preacher back in the day. A week or so passed and we went to a church potluck dinner, and it just so happened that Larry was there with Roberta. We introduced ourselves and he put up a gruff front, but I could tell he was someone I could get along with. By the end of that dinner, I was teasing him that I had been warned about him, but he didn't scare me. He cracked a smile, and we were friends at that point. Roberta was tickled, as they say in the south, and we had a lunch invitation to come to their home that week.

Over pimento cheese sandwiches we talked with Larry for the first time about the Church. He knew a lot about Joseph Smith and the basic teachings of the Church, enough, he felt, to warrant his conviction that it wasn't true. We weren't the first missionaries Roberta had invited over but, in that conversation, we learned that Larry had never actually committed to taking the lessons. With encouragement from us and maybe a kick under the table from Roberta, Larry reluctantly agreed to commit to the lessons. We agreed we'd come back a few days later.

Our next couple of lessons went ok but Larry really knew the Bible and seemed set on refuting most of what we taught. We were nervous before each lesson that we wouldn't have answers to Larry's questions, especially because he had such extensive knowledge of the Bible and had read some negative literature regarding Joseph Smith and the Restoration. At the end of our 2nd or 3rd lesson Larry told us that he appreciated what we had to say, and he could tell we were sincere but he just couldn't accept it for himself because there simply wasn't any evidence. There was a pause and without thinking much I said, "Larry, can you catch?" and I tossed him a blue copy of the Book of Mormon. "That's the evidence!"

We opened to the back of the Book of Mormon and read Moroni 10:3–5 with him. We then challenged him to read and pray to know if the Book of Mormon was true. When we returned for our next lesson, we began with our regular small talk and then transitioned into teaching our lesson. The end of our lesson hadn't left me feeling very hopeful about Larry following through on reading and praying about the Book of Mormon, so I almost forgot to follow up and ask him. Casually I asked if he had read and prayed about the Book of Mormon since we had last met. There was a long pause and then I heard him mumble something. I had to ask him to repeat himself and almost couldn't believe what I heard.

"I think it's true," he said quietly followed by a not-so-quiet squeal from Roberta.

Larry's testimony of the Book of Mormon was the catapult for his testimony of the restored gospel, Joseph Smith, and The Church of Jesus Christ of Latter-day Saints. Everything changed that day and he began to embrace the gospel. He made difficult changes gracefully as he prepared for baptism. I will never forget the day he was baptized. The small room was packed with people. Larry chose to speak, and I don't think I will ever forget the feeling I had as he shared his testimony that day.

Larry's conversion to the gospel illustrates the simple truth that the Book of Mormon can speak for itself. Too often we spend time discussing the Book of Mormon without opening it up and letting it do the heavy lifting. Larry had read many anti-Latter-day Saint books telling him what the Book of Mormon was. On many occasions, he heard his wife and several sets of missionaries and ward members testify of the truthfulness of the Book of Mormon. However, it wasn't until Larry sincerely read it for himself that he realized the Book of Mormon was of God. With this testimony, he had the courage to be baptized and share the gospel with others, even though it was contrary to everything he previously believed.

We flew to Nashville with our daughter after her mission to attend the temple when Larry received his own endowment. While sitting down to some Southern food at a local restaurant, I asked Larry how he felt about his experience. He said he was embarrassed that he had the truth in his house for seven years and missed it. Why? Because he relied on what others had said about the Book of Mormon instead of reading it for himself.

In June of 2017 at a mission president seminar, Elder D. Todd Christofferson shared the following about the Book of Mormon: "Given, then, that the power of the Book of Mormon comes as we allow the book to speak for itself, the question for you is, how will your missionaries get people to read the Book of Mormon and also to pray with real intent about its truthfulness?"[13]

---

13. D. Todd Christofferson, quoted in Amanda K. Fronk, "An Experiment Upon the Word," *BYU Magazine*, spring 2018, https://magazine.byu.edu/article/an-experiment-upon-the-word/.

CHAPTER 15: LET THE BOOK SPEAK FOR ITSELF

When sharing the Book of Mormon with a friend, we should remember the end goal. We are not just trying to muster the courage to pass out a copy of the book. The goal is to inspire them to read its words. *Preach My Gospel* says, "Have confidence that the Holy Ghost will testify to anyone who reads and ponders the Book of Mormon and asks God if it is true with a sincere heart, real intent, and faith in Christ."[14] Our job is to inspire others to want to read—the Book of Mormon will do the rest of the work!

One straightforward way to help people interact with the words of the Book of Mormon is to share specific passages on social media. Obviously, we do not want to post all seventy-seven verses of Jacob's allegory of the olive tree. But we can share simple, powerful, and Christ-centered phrases that provide enough room for the Spirit to do the work.

Another way to let the Book of Mormon speak for itself is to invite people into spaces or activities where the words of the Book of Mormon are read and studied. For example, asking people to stay for family prayer where a short scripture passage is read from the Book of Mormon is one way to help people experience the power of the word. Maybe inviting someone to Sunday School, an institute class, or a sacrament meeting will allow the Book of Mormon to spark faith.

Another simple way to help people make contact with the actual text of the Book of Mormon is to use specific passages to answer questions. So often, when people inquire about our beliefs, they ask questions that the Book of Mormon can answer. For example, can you think of verses that answer these questions:

1. How do you know there is a God?
2. What does your church teach about racial equality?
3. Why do you believe in the Book of Mormon?
4. Isn't faith just believing without evidence?
5. Doesn't following a church's standards lead to a loss of freedom?

Opportunities will arise as we think of ways to help others read the Book of Mormon. The main goal should be to allow people to spend time with the book rather than trying to convince people it's

---

14. *Preach My Gospel: A Guide to Missionary Service* (2019), 103.

true. Stephen Anjum is a fitting example of this principle. His life changed forever when he asked to borrow the book and began to read it for himself.

As Stephen and his family navigated those challenging years as refugees in England, my family was growing and expanding and I was engaged in my career as a full-time seminary and institute teacher for the Church. I found many occasions to share Stephen's story in the context of the lessons I was teaching to my students. They were interested in the story, and many were deeply inspired by Stephen's example. Through the years, many of my students wrote letters to the Anjums.

As refugees in England, the Anjums felt halted. It seemed like their days of church leadership and phenomenal missionary success were over and that their life had mostly been reduced to survival. However, in America, their story was inspiring many, and I loved telling Stephen about the impact he was still having.

In October of 2015, I received a phone call that changed our lives forever. Elder Jeffrey R. Holland's secretary was on the line and invited M'Shelle and me to come to his office for a visit. That inspiring interview with Elder Holland led to another interview with President Henry B. Eyring, where M'Shelle and I were called to serve as mission leaders for the Church. President Eyring looked into my soul and discerned what I needed to hear as he called me and gave me needed counsel. We knew that we were in the presence of a prophet of God and a special witness of Jesus Christ. We were on holy ground that day, and the lessons we learned from him will never be forgotten.

A month later, we found out we would be serving in the California Redlands Mission. Our oldest two children, Lisie and Jared, were home from their missions and attending BYU. Our third child, Rob, subsequently received his mission call to the Spain Barcelona Mission and ended up coming to California with us for one month before leaving. Our youngest two sons, Brad and Scott, were fourteen and twelve and joined us on our missionary journey for the next three years.

The lessons I had learned about the power of the Book of Mormon to gather scattered Israel came with me into the mission field. I knew that if we could get the people of California to read the Book of Mormon, it would change their lives forever. To inspire our

CHAPTER 15: LET THE BOOK SPEAK FOR ITSELF

missionaries and teach them about the power of the Book of Mormon as the instrument of the harvest, I invited the Anjum family to join a round of zone conferences via Zoom. Stephen and I were able to share his conversion story together. It was an honor to teach those powerful principles to our missionaries with Stephen as my missionary companion on each of those days.

Repeatedly, through our experiences as mission leaders and our friendship with the Anjums, I have learned to rely less on my own words and let the Book of Mormon do the talking.

16

THE REUNION

IN DECEMBER OF 2021, WHILE AT HOME IN BIRMINGHAM, ENGLAND, Stephen received word that his sister Aster had suddenly passed away back in Pakistan. Despite tight financial circumstances, Stephen and Thomsena decided they needed to return to Faisalabad to honor his sister's life and console her family.

While in Pakistan, besides attending the funeral, Stephen and Thomsena had the chance to go to the wedding of Thomsena's niece. The wedding was held at a Catholic church in Warispura. As is customary in Pakistan, the guests of the bride sat on one side of the room and the guests of the groom sat on the other.

As Stephen sat down, he looked across the aisle and noticed a familiar face from the past. There sat the pastor who had given him my copy of the Book of Mormon thirty-three years earlier and then took it back.

Stephen wanted to meet the pastor and reintroduce himself after all those years in hopes that he could find out what became of the book. The opportunity had now unexpectedly presented itself. After the ceremony, Stephen approached him and introduced himself. The pastor looked into Stephen's eyes, gave him a big smile, and said, "How can I forget you?" The pastor told Stephen that he remembered him and was waiting for this time when they could meet again. The pastor then invited Stephen to come to his church and school the next morning. "You will be our chief guest," he said. "Tomorrow is also the annual result day at the school, and it would be an honor for us if you could distribute the children's results."

Early in the morning, Stephen and Thomsena, along with their Tamir charity staff, showed up at the pastor's church and were invited into his office. As the pastor sat at his desk, Stephen could not help looking beyond the pastor at the medium-sized bookshelf behind him. His eyes scanned the shelves until he spotted a blue paperback book. The pastor stepped away for a few minutes and left the Anjums alone there in the office. Stephen immediately went to the bookshelf and pulled down the blue paperback book. Sure enough, it was the Book of Mormon—the very one that had been taken from him. Stephen opened the book and saw the paper with my testimony and return address. After more than three decades, he was once again holding the book that changed his life.

Stephen later jokingly shared that in that moment, he felt like Nephi trying to figure out how to get the plates from Laban! He placed the book back on the shelf and returned to his chair nervously waiting for the pastor to return.

When the pastor came back into the room, he invited the Anjums to join him as his special guests at an assembly for the students in his school. At the assembly, the pastor gave Stephen and Thomsena flowers and presented the couple to the students. Stephen sat on the stand and was asked to speak to the students and was honored for his charitable contributions to the community. He wondered why he was being treated with such respect from a man who he remembered being an antagonist of the Church.

Following the meeting, the pastor took the Anjums on a tour of the campus and the nearby city streets. He pointed out that many people living on the streets were addicted to drugs and alcohol. The Anjums were eventually invited to the pastor's home for a special meal. Stephen and Thomsena were amazed to be served a rooster raised organically on a farm. This is a sign of profound respect according to Pakistani custom.

After the meal ended, the Anjums were taken back to the pastor's office. When they all sat down, the pastor walked over to his shelf and pulled down the copy of the Book of Mormon. He held the book in his hand and told Stephen that he had held this book for all those years and kept it safe, knowing that Stephen would one day return and ask for it. In the early years of his ministry, the pastor told Stephen that he would track down the young, native Pakistani missionaries of the Church and warn them to beware of the book and The Church of Jesus Christ of Latter-day Saints. He did all he could to dissuade them from continuing forward with their membership in the Church.

However, over time he noticed something. Members of the Church quit smoking and drinking. The pastor watched their lives blossom, and he saw the fruits of their new faith. In contrast to the lives of those on the street, which he had just shown the Anjums, the pastor realized this new church was transforming lives. In time, rather than warn people about the Church, he began to have a profound respect for what the Church was doing for the people in his community. The pastor soon recognized that the book was not evil but was drawing people to the Savior. He felt an impression that God wanted him to preserve the book and eventually get it back into the hands of Stephen.

The moment had come, and he handed the book to Stephen, cheering aloud and clapping as if to rejoice that he had completed an important task from the Lord.

They laughed and enjoyed the moment together. Stephen thanked the pastor for his kindness and the role that he played in bringing the Book of Mormon to so many Pakistani people. Little did the young aspiring Christian pastor know, back in the late 1980s when he met two missionaries from the Church in Bristol, England, that the book they gave him would launch the Church in his hometown of Faisalabad and transform countless lives throughout Pakistan. He was an unknowing instrument in the hands of the Lord to help gather Israel.

Ironically, the same book that flew to Pakistan from England in 1988 in the suitcase of a young pastor now flew from Pakistan back to England in 2021 in the suitcase of Stephen Anjum. When Stephen got back home, he wrote a message to me on WhatsApp (a long way from having his dad type out a message on their old typewriter) telling of the miraculous events of his trip back to Pakistan.

When I woke up in the United States, I turned off my alarm and saw a WhatsApp notification. I knew that it would either be from Stephen or Razzaq Gill. I opened the notification and read the remarkable story of Stephen being reunited with the book. I became lost in the memories of the events that started with my mom walking out to the mailbox on a spring morning in Provo, Utah, so many years ago. I thanked the Lord for His goodness and for the privilege of being an instrument in His hands.

We arranged for a video call, and I was met with the warm smiles of my friends Stephen and Thomsena Anjum. Stephen held up the book and rejoiced, "Here it is!" He zoomed in on the paper with my testimony, and at age fifty-one, I saw the message from my eighteen-year-old self.

Stephen started thumbing through the pages and showed me the verses he marked when he first got the book and talked about his experience discovering those truths for the first time. Along with many other passages, he remembers especially being taken in by Nephi's words in 1 Nephi 10 and Moroni's great sermon on faith, hope, and charity in Moroni 7. It was inspiring to hear him share his love and testimony of the Book of Mormon.

As I reflect on this experience, I am reminded of the prophecy made in the blessing Stephen received from Robert Simmons while he was confirmed a member of the Church:

> I confirmed Stephen a member of the Church. . . . [He received] a beautiful blessing in which he was promised that as he remained faithful, he would be an instrument in the hands of the Lord in bringing many, many people into the Church; he would be sealed in the temple; and he would teach the gospel in this land and in others.

All those promises were fulfilled in remarkable ways. Our loving Heavenly Father is aware of each of His children. God knew in 1988 that one of his noble and great ones living in Pakistan was prepared for the gospel and would be used as an instrument in His hands in doing a mighty work. When the Lord wants something done, He can work through small means to bring great things to pass. As Alma 37:6–7 says:

> Now ye may suppose that this is foolishness in me; but behold I say unto you, that by small and simple things are great things brought to pass; and small means in many instances doth confound the wise.
>
> And the Lord God doth work by means to bring about his great and eternal purposes; and by very small means the Lord doth confound the wise and bringeth about the salvation of many souls.

The call given by President Ezra Taft Benson back in 1988 to "flood the earth with the Book of Mormon," which led to the conversion of Stephen Anjum and many others, was renewed by Elder Ronald R. Rasband in the October 2022 general conference. I close with his words:

> My dear friends, as an Apostle of the Lord, I invite you to follow our beloved prophet, President Nelson, in flooding the earth with the Book of Mormon. The need is so great; we need to act now. I promise that you will be participating in "the greatest work on earth," the gathering of Israel, as you are inspired to reach out to those who have been "kept from the truth because they know not where to find it." They need your testimony and witness of how this book has changed your life and drawn you closer to God, His peace, and His "tidings of great joy."[15]

---

15. Ronald R. Rasband, "This Day," *Liahona*, Nov. 2022, 27.

Epilogue

One day, Stephen and Thomsena messaged me to let me know that they were selected to represent their former charity at a conference in Vancouver, Canada. Their flights would be paid for by the organization. Stephen and I saw this as a great chance to get him and Thomsena, as well as Sharoon and Ray, to Utah for the first time.

After we picked the Anjums up at the airport and arrived at our home, we all gathered in our downstairs family room and began to talk and share memories. This was only our second time being together in person.

Stephen said, "Sean, I have the book—do you want to see it?" He then placed back into my hands the Book of Mormon I had sent out thirty-three years earlier. Here is what I wrote in the front cover all those years before:

"I know that this book is a true history. I know the Book of Mormon to be true. I know that Joseph Smith was a true prophet of God. I know that the he translated this book. I know that the Mormon Church is true. I hope that you will read it and pray about it and the Lord will give you a feeling that it is true. P.S. I'm praying for you."

From Provo to England to Pakistan, back to England, and back to Provo.

Appendix

Below is a record of some of the letters Sean and Stephen exchanged.

Stephen's First Letter to Sean

Dear Sean,

My name is Stephen Anjum and I am a Pakistani Christian. Some times ago I came to know about you and, (the Book of Mormon) Another Testament of Jesus Christ. I went through the Holy book and found that this is real book of God. I believe that Mormon church is true and I also believe that Joseph Smith was a True Prophet of God. I believe that it is a gift of God. I hope that anyone, who will read it and pray will get blessing of God.

Dear Sean, I wish to be preacher of Holy Mormon. I want to get more knowledge about Mormon. Please send me some books in easy English related to Mormons. If you have any representative in Pakistan then inform me so that I may get more information from him. I hope you will accept my friendship. My mailing address is as:

YOUR BROTHER IN CHRIST,
Stephen Anjum

APPENDIX

Sean's First Letter to Stephen

Dear Stephen,

I was so happy to receive your letter. I see that the Book of Mormon has a great influence on you. It has influenced me in the same way. I love it so much. I know that it is a true book. I was very surprised to find out that my book made it all the way to Pakistan. I wrote my testimony in it hoping that it would find someone and change their life. I was so excited to see that my prayers have been answered. I know that our Heavenly Father wanted you to receive this book. It is a true miracle. It is definitely a gift of God. Without Him everything would be impossible.

I love our Heavenly Father and Jesus Christ so much. Without Jesus we could not be saved to live with him and our Heavenly Father again some day. Your words inspired me. Let me tell you a little bit about myself. I am 18 years old. I have lived in Provo, Utah all of my life. The headquarters of the Mormon Church are in Salt Lake City, Utah. That is very near my home. The church now has over 6 million people. That is probably amazing to you. It is one of the fastest growing churches. The church was organized in 1830 by the Prophet Joseph Smith. I have enclosed the Joseph Smith Story in this package.

Read it and pray to our Heavenly Father to know that it is true. I know it is. I have been raised in the church all of my life. It is a great organization. At the age of 19 members of the church are encouraged to serve a mission for the Lord. On missions we seek to find people like you who are looking for the truth. Missionaries are trained to teach people. Unfortunately the church cannot send missionaries to your country. Tomorrow, I will talk to a man who knows the situation in Pakistan and he will tell me how to have a representative of the church find you. I will tell you this information at the end of my letter. I have received my mission call because I will turn 19 in one month. I have been asked to go to Toronto, Canada. I will first go to the Missionary Training Center where I will be better trained. I have also been asked to learn Spanish so that I can speak to the Spanish speakers there.

I am so excited to teach people the truth. I love the Lord and want to serve him well. I want to help to teach you about the truth through my letters. I pray that the Holy Ghost will fill your soul as I write to you. That is how people are converted to the church.

Stephen, as missionaries we have an organized plan of how to teach the truth. It is broken into 6 parts called discussions. Each letter I will give you the basics of each discussion about the church. The first discussion is called "The Plan of our Heavenly Father." I will give it to you now.

Most people believe in a supreme being, even though they may call him by different names. We know that God lives. He is perfect, all wise and all powerful. He is also kind and just. I know he lives. He is my Father in Heaven. We are created in his image. (Genesis 1:26–27) (Acts 17:24–29). That makes me and you brothers. God has a plan for us because he loves us. He wants us to live with him again. His plan shows how we can accomplish this. Without his help we could not make it. We are all human so we sin. God sent Jesus Christ to help us overcome sin (Read John 3:16) (1 Nephi 11:32–33) Jesus did this through his sacrifice and resurrection for us. I love him so much for that. Without it, I would be nothing.

I was excited to learn that you are Christian. I'm sure you love Christ. We need to have faith to do what Jesus has taught. God has revealed this plan to us. He has a pattern of doing this. First, he chooses witnesses. They are righteous men that learn from first hand experience about the truth. These men are called prophets and apostles. Second, the prophets testify of Christ through their words and also through scripture (The Bible and the Book of Mormon) Third, the Holy Ghost confirms the truth. The Holy Ghost can be felt within you. It is a warm feeling. A feeling of better understanding. I know that you have felt this by the words you wrote to me. Fourth, we are invited to obey. We are invited to obey the words of the prophets that we hear and read in scripture. Read Amos 3:7, Moroni 7:29–32.

The prophet Joseph Smith is a modern witness of Christ. God followed his pattern for revealing truth in our day by choosing Joseph Smith. Read the Joseph Smith story that I have enclosed. It talks about how he was confused about religion. Then how he learned to gain wisdom (James 1:5), how he prayed for wisdom, and how he saw God the Father, and his son Jesus Christ. I know that he was a prophet of God. I was excited to read that you know this too.

As a witness of Christ, Joseph Smith translated the Book of Mormon by the power of God. It is truly an inspired book. I know that it truly testifies of Christ's visit to America. I am pleased that you have read it and know that it is true. The Holy Ghost witnesses to us that it is true if we pray about it and have faith. I know that it's true.

Stephen, I'm sure that you have many questions and I would love to help you answer them. I have many books that I will send you to help you learn more. Each letter I will teach you a new discussion. I love you very much.

Stephen, to join the Mormon church you must be baptized. As soon as we can get someone with authority to contact you, will you be baptized? With your strong testimony I know you can influence many people in Pakistan.

Please write me and tell me all about yourself. How old are you? How did you receive the Book of Mormon that I sent? Tell me about your family? (I am in a family of 5 kids, I am second to youngest) Tell me about Pakistan and everything. I consider you a great friend. You will be in my prayers. Trust in the Lord and he will find someone that will contact you in Pakistan. I know it. I pray that you will desire to be baptized.

May the Lord bless you,

Your brother in Christ,

Sean Dixon

PS - Stephen - Teach the people in Pakistan about the Book of Mormon

Second Letter from Stephen Anjum: June 6, 1989

Dear S. Dixon

Greeting from Pakistan. I am very happy to receive your letter and precious gift which you sent for me three week ago. Yes, of course, the Mormon Book has a great influence on me and I love it so much. You will be pleased that I have introduce this book to my best friends. My friends also show strong interest in this church. The book "A Marvelous Work and a Wonder" and other books are really gift of God. I am sorry I could not write you soon due to domestic problems. Dear Dixon being a Christian I love Jesus Christ and the Heavenly Father. You have asked me about myself so, I am 24 years old. I have passed recently my Graduation (B.Sc) exam from Punjab University of Pakistan, which is the top most Universities in Pakistan.

Sean, Pakistan is a poor and developing country. There are no good jobs for me at present so I am teaching in a St. Paul's High School as a science teacher on very poor salary. Dear Sean, I love teaching and study. In the case of education, Pakistan is very backward. My Father is clerk in Standard Chartered Bank Faisalabad. When I was sixteen my mother died. Later on, on 25th March 1984, my father got into an accident and his left leg was fractured and infected. It's God's miracle that my father was cured after four years. Financially we became poor, because it was very hard for my father to pull a large family. We are ten brothers and sisters. I am the eldest one. During disease period my father continue help me in my study. During this period I did F. SC and B.Sc. Similarly my other brothers and sister continue their study.

Sean, I got "The Book of Mormon" from my college fellow. . . . He gave this book to study. [His] brother is a pastor. During training in England, he brought this book from England. So when I study yours testimony and the testimony of prophet Joseph Smith I felt that is Holy Ghost guiding me to study further and further. Then it revealed on me that Joseph Smith is true prophet of God. I felt that it is a Holy Ghost guiding me to accept Mormon. Sean, I believe that "The Book of Mormon" is a true book. Dear, unfortunately few days ago my class fellow had taken back his book and at present I have no book.

Sean, I am very thankful to you for your teaching. I have few friend when they visit to my house we discuss over "The Plan of Our Heavenly Father" and the blessing which our Heavenly Father has bestowed to prophet Joseph Smith. I know that its not your or I doing this work but it is a Holy Spirit who is doing this work to fulfill the plan of God.

Sean, as you say, that you could not send missionaries to our country. What's the reason? So how can I trained to learn or to teach people? Because I feel that I have not complete knowledge about church and I need training. Sean, is it possible that I came to your country for higher training or in Toronto, Canada. Also, still no body has came to see me here. Let me know how many Pakistani members are in our church.

You asked about Pakistan. So Pakistan is a Islamic country and Christians are minority here. Although Pakistan is a developing country but it is a beautiful country by all means. It's a agricultural country. All kinds of Agricultural products are grown here. The most historical city in Pakistan is Lahore. Islamabad City is the Capital of Pakistan. This city is as beautiful as Switzerland. Karachi is the biggest city by population and by industrial. It is also important due to big seaport on Arabic Ocean. My city Faisalabad is also industrial city. Sean, few days ago, I saw news about Mormon in newspaper that 2 Mormon missionaries named Todd Ray Wilson, 19, of Wellington, Utah, and Jeffrey Brent Ball, 21, from Coalville, Utah, died in a hail of submachine gun fire on the doorstep of their home. I became very sad to learn this news. I pray that may God rest their soul in peace. Let me know what was the matter.

Sean, I shall be very very thankful to you if you send "The Book of Mormons" and the Holy Bible. (IF possible). OK, I send my letter with best wishes that our God help you by all means especially during your training in Toronto Canada. Pay my best compliment to your parents, brothers and Sisters and the President of the Church Ezra Taft Benson.

Thank you
Cordially Yours
Stephen Anjum

Sean's Second Letter to Stephen: June 21, 1989

(This was sent in a box filled with copies of the Book of Mormon and other Church books.)

Dear Stephen-

I was excited to get your letter. I was so filled with joy to know that a Book of Mormon I sent touched someone's life. I know it wasn't me, but it was the power of the Book of Mormon and the Holy Ghost that helped you to believe it was true. Thanks for telling me all about you. I was really interested to find out how you received the Book of Mormon. Stephen, I know God wanted you to have that book. You are a chosen person. God directed that book to you I really believe. I was also very happy to know that when you received it you shared it with your friends. You are a missionary if you will share the truth of the Book of Mormon with others. I receive much joy when I share the Book of Mormon and that is why I am on a mission right now. I want to tell everybody about the gospel of Jesus Christ.

I am in the Missionary Training Center in Provo, Utah and in 5 days I will be in Toronto Canada ready to teach people there. I read your letter to the missionaries here and they were thrilled and very happy. It always strengthens others beliefs when they here stories of people like you who believe in the Book of Mormon and want to share it. I have some friends who want to send you some more Book of Mormons for your friends. I have given you in this box the Book of Mormon, the Bible, the Doctrine and Covenants and Pearl of Great Price which are additional revelations given to Joseph Smith. These books are what we as Mormons call "The Standard Works" (Bible, Book of Mormon, Doctrine and Covenants, Pearl of Great Price). I think you will really enjoy them all.

I have also enclosed a magazine about our temples. We have temples all over the world for worthy members of the church to attend. You can read the magazine to find out more about temples. In temples, people can be married for time and all eternity. Your whole family can live together forever because of Temple marriage. I am so thankful for this because I love my family so much. We just need to be worthy.

Also every April and October the Mormon Church has a general conference that is broadcasted to different parts of the world. I have given you the magazine called the "Ensign" that has the talks of President Ezra Taft Benson and the other General Authorities of the church. In the middle of the magazine there is pictures of President Benson, our prophet, and all the Apostles of our church. They are the greatest men. In the Missionary Training Center I have had a chance to personally hear these men speak about the gospel. The Spirit is so strong when they speak.

I have also given you pamphlets that explain different things. The pamphlet called "The gospel of Jesus Christ" is an outline of the second missionary discussion. The first was "The Plan of Our Heavenly Father." There are six in total and I will keep sending them to you. Everyone is so excited to hear about you. I have enclosed some letters from people who live by me. Some are adults and some are little children.

Thanks for telling me about your life. That is neat that you come from a big family. I have one brother and 3 sisters and a Mom and Dad. My brother and two of my sisters are married. I am the second to youngest. That's neat that you are a science teacher. You seem very smart to me.

I talked to a man and he said he is going to send your letter to a General Authority who will tell a person to find you and your friends. I will be praying that they can talk to you as soon as possible. You need to pray a lot also so this can happen. Try to prepare as many people as possible to read the Book of Mormon so they can receive the great blessings also. I know that people will contact you. The church has many missionaries all over the world, but unfortunately there are still places where our missionaries cannot go. It is mostly because of political reasons with countries and they don't allow missionaries in. Eventually that will change and before long the whole world will have a chance to hear the gospel and be baptized. We all need to pray for that.

Those two missionaries that you read about died in LaPaz Bolivia. It was a real sad story to hear about. But I know the Lord will bless them in Heaven for their dedication as missionaries. Read Alma 60:13 in the Book of Mormon and that might help to explain why that happened. That is a very rare case and for the most part our missionaries are experiencing great success. There are now over 6 million members of our church throughout the world and it is getting bigger and bigger all the time. Keep writing me back and asking all the questions you can think of and I will try to answer them for you. Read these books I have sent you and you will gain greater knowledge. I want to help you.

Please continue to write and tell me how the work is going in Pakistan. How many people who have gained a knowledge that the Mormon church is true. I will pray for you. May God bless you as you share the truths of the Mormon Church. May he bless you that someone will contact you. Tell our friends my best wishes and your family also. As I get your letters I will continue to send you more information and letters. Thanks again for your letter. You have helped me to gain a stronger knowledge because of your great attitude. I know Jesus Christ is my Savior. I know that the Book of Mormon is true and that Joseph Smith was a true Prophet. I also know that Ezra Taft Benson is a true Prophet today and he leads the Church through revelation from Jesus Christ. Best wishes to you in your goal of getting more knowledge.

Your Brother in Christ,

Sean Dixon

Letter from Stephen to Sean: July 10, 1990

Dear Dixon,

How are you? I received your letter dated June 9, 90. I am very thankful to you for writing me. Dear, I can never never forget you and the Book of Mormon. I can never never forget your love, teaching, guidance and every thing you sent to me - I can never forget the love of your friends.

Really, I have no words to express my feeling for you and your friends those who wrote me their testimonies. Thank you very much for sending me treasure of books. I really enjoyed them very much. Dear Sean, I really need your love and guidance. It is because of your testimony, I got the truthfulness of the world. I bear my testimony that Joseph Smith is a true prophet of God and "The Book of Mormon" is revealed Book of God which supplement the Bible.

Sean, you would be glad to hear that the President of Asia Area Centre Hong Kong has contacted me, they often wrote me letter for guidance. I have informed them all the situation of members in Pakistan - Now there are 32 families who takes keen interest in this Church.

Sean, we will highly welcome you and other missionaries in Pakistan. Recently, Merlin R. Libbert, 2nd counselor from Hong Kong has sent me list of the members of Mormon Church living in Pakistan. I am very happy to find all of them - Now I can share my religious terms with them. I have wrote them letter but still nobody has contact to me.

Dear Sean, it's my heartest wish that I got baptize by your hands - After so much consideration and pray I have decided to get baptism of this Holy and true church. You always find me a strong member of Mormon Church. It's all because of power of Book of Mormon; I got the mystery of life and love. Sean, I could not express my happiness and affection for the pretty and innocent testimonies of small kids and young. Whenever I read the testimonies of kids and young, they encourage [me] and make me bold. I am boast that I am Mormon. I have tried to translate some pamphlet into local "Urdu" language. Sean, in other separate letter I shall write to you how much I have to suffer trial and problem a past year. OK, God bless you:

Yours in Christ,
Stephen Anjum

Letter from Sean to Stephen from Toronto, Canada: July 21, 1990

Dear Stephen,

I was so excited and happy to receive your last letter. I shared the letter with the other missionaries that work with me here. They were amazed at how the Lord guided the Book of Mormon into your hands. It is truly a sign that the Lord wants the true gospel preached to every person in every country in the world. Missionaries from our church are now preparing to go into Russia and they are already in many of the eastern European countries. I hope and pray that soon missionaries will also be able to come into Pakistan and preach the gospel to your countrymen.

I was so excited to hear that you have decided to be baptized. I promise you that you have made the right decision. I was also very happy to learn that there are 32 families that are very interested in the church. I know that the Lord will bless you as you continue to spread his word to your friends and family members. I am glad that the area presidency has made contact with you. They will be able to tell you how and when you can be baptized. I will write another letter to them.

My heart is so full of joy to know that you have come to find out for yourself that these things are true. Lasting peace and happiness can only be found through the gospel of Christ. Because of your strong testimony of the Book of Mormon you will be a great help to the church. You will be able play a big role in getting the church started in Pakistan.

It sounds like you have had many trials and problems in the last year. Many times when we find truth we also get opposition. Make sure that you continue to pray to our Heavenly Father for guidance and I know he will bless you and help you in all that you do.

I wish you the best of luck in all that you do. Thanks again for writing back to me. I would love to be able to hear from you again soon. If there is anything I can help you with I will be happy to do it. Just write and tell me what you need. Do you need more Book of Mormon for your friends? May God bless you as you continue to learn more about his gospel.

Your brother in Christ,

Sean Dixon

Letter from Stephen to Sean: September 21, 1990

Dear Dixon,

How are you? I cannot tell you what great joy my family member, and myself had when we received your letter and the magazine "The Ensign". However going through the letter we felt your great love for us. Yes, we understood that Baptism is indispensable sacrament for our souls - The Branch President here in Islamabad Branch has contacted with me - He has invited me for religious meeting. Soon, I will go Islamabad to meet with them. The branch President Rick Smith wrote me excitedly that where and how I have join the church. He is also interested to know about the other members. I just got back from village after few week. I spent those days with my friend living in different places. I had also chance to visit a desert area called Cholistan. There I saw many peoples who have not yet got the voice of God. They are neither Christian nor Muslims. I have plan to go in that are to teach them.

Sean, Area Presidency Hong Kong who sent me booklet in Urdu printed in U.S.A. Nowadays, I am seeking for new job. Due to low salary and prejudice among the teachers, I have to left the teaching from school. Yesterday I had interview in a medical company for the post of medical representative of the company. If I get this job I have to visit 12 town around my to introduce the company product. Brother, its my heartiest wish to become a Church representative not a medical representative. You have write me that if there is any thing I can help you will be happy to do it. I sincerely need your help as my younger brother Sebastian Javed and me want to join the missionary training center like you. If you can do anything this connection then write me please. Secondly, if possible send me video cassettes related to Mormon Church and 10 Books of Mormon in English or Urdu. Nowaday, my father is invalid due to fractured in leg once again. Please pray for early recovery of my father. OK, Good bye

Yours,

Stephen Anjum

Letter from Sean to Stephen from Toronto, Canada: October 27, 1990

Dear Stephen,

Thank you very much for your letter. I always look forward to hearing from you and your progress. I am so happy to know that the branch president and the area presidency are in contact with you. I hope and pray that soon you will be able to be baptized along with many of your family and friends. After you are baptized you will receive the gift of the Holy Ghost by the laying on of hands. This gift will be a great help to you in your life.

I am sorry to hear that your economic situation is not very good, as you have had to change jobs I hope you will find success as a medical representative.

It sounds like you are a great missionary as you have been sharing the gospel with friends and family. You can be a very big help to the growth of the church in Pakistan, as missionaries, such as myself, still aren't permitted to preach the gospel there. You asked me if there is anything I can do to help you and your brother join the missionary training center. In order to be a full time missionary you will have to wait 1 year from the time you are baptized. The branch president there should be able to tell you exactly what needs to happen for you to become a missionary. In the mean time, you can be a missionary in your country.

The church is growing very rapidly and is spreading into many more nations (Czechoslovakia, Poland, Hungary, Russia, etc.) We have been given the truth so we have great responsibility to share it. I look forward to hearing from you again. I pray for your father that he will have a speedy recovery. You will be in my prayers.

Your brother,

Sean Dixon

Letter from Sean to Stephen: January 14, 1991

Dear Stephen,

Thanks so much for your Christmas card. It was so great to hear from you again. I was so happy to hear that you were able to meet with different members of the branch there. Were you able to get baptized yet? I sure hope so.

I sent a package with several Book of Mormons and a video cassette with videos about the church on it back in November. I hope that it has arrived safely to you. I hope this letter finds you happy and doing well and progressing in the gospel. I often think about you and I pray that the gospel will be made fully available to you soon.

I am nearing the end of my mission here in Toronto and have fully enjoyed my time here so far. I have been able to teach the gospel to many people and see them accept it and get baptized. This type of work brings so much joy and happiness! There are many people here from India and Pakistan and all countries of the world.

I hope the conflict in the middle east won't affect you and the people of Pakistan. It's sad to see people that have to turn to war. I will return to my home in Utah in June of '91 to attend university, etc. Thanks for your great friendship. I sincerely hope and pray that someday I will be able to meet you personally. If you have an extra picture of yourself, please send it with your next letter. Thanks again for everything.

Your brother in Christ,

Sean

PS - Read 2 Nephi 31:20; Helaman 5:12

Letter from Stephen to Sean: February 25, 1991

Dear Sean,

Hellow, I hope things are going well for you - Thank you very much for nice letter and thoughtfulness. Yes, I am preparing myself for baptism. There are some more people who are waiting for baptism - Nowaday I am learning Gospel Principles Manual with some of my friends. Now we hope to be able to get baptise soon. The members of the church have been temporarily evacuated due to Gulf War and tension. But Robert Simmons, one of the members

APPENDIX

of church is here. We are connected each other by corresponding. Next month I will go personally to see him in Islamabad.

Thank you very much for sending us books and video cassettes. Which I have not yet received. I think that this package would take some more days to reach to me. Bro as you know people of Pakistan make arrange marriage for their children. My family members have also choose a girl as my better half. She is teaching in a local school. My family want to make my marriage in the month of July. But I am not willing to this decision because of present I have not proper job and secondly I believe as it is written in the Gospel Principle that eternal marriage is essential for our exaltation now as well as in the eternities. It is my heartest wish that I could make temple marriage. I would be very happy if you wrote me about eternal marriage and its blessing. I am sending my photograph to you. I believe that we will be able to convert many souls into the true church of Jesus Christ of Latter day Saint. Pay our best compliments to all your companions. Thank you very much for precious unity and love.

Your brother in Jesus, Stephen Anjum

Letter from Sean to Stephen: April 2, 1991

Dear Stephen,

I just received your letter. It was so good to hear from you again. I am still so amazed and happy that our Heavenly Father led the Book of Mormon into your hands. It has really helped to strengthen my testimony of the gospel. I have shared your story with many of my missionary companions and they are all so thrilled to know how the Lord works to expand the gospel into all nations of the world. There was a family from India from the Sikh faith that were recently converted and baptized. They have strong testimonies of the gospel and we use them to go around and teach people of their own culture. The Lord is definitely gathering his elect.

I know you have been called by the Lord to do a great work there in Pakistan. I am so happy that there are many who are interested in the gospel. Keep up the great work. I was impressed by your knowledge of the gospel. Yes, eternal marriage is very important and is something that can be made available one year after your baptism. Your wife would also need to be baptized for at least one year. That is a wonderful goal to shoot for and one I know you will never regret. The thought of living together with your wife and kids is a wonderful one. I know that is what I am planning on. My Dad and Mom were married in the temple and because of that our family can live together as long as we are all worthy and faithful in our lives. A civil marriage is only valid until death do you part. However, a couple who have been civilly married can be sealed together in the temple.

I am nearing the end of my 2-year mission in Toronto. I will be going home to Utah at the 1st of June. This mission has been a wonderful experience for me. I have seen the Spirit of the Lord touch many people. The Church is growing and expanding all over the earth as prophesied in the Bible. Here in Toronto, I have met people from all over the world. I have been very cultured over these past 2 years.

Well Stephen, I wish you all the best. May the Lord's richest blessings be upon you and your family and the members of the church in Pakistan.

Your brother in Christ

Sean Dixon

LETTER FROM STEPHEN TO SEAN: MAY 28, 1991

Greeting from Pakistan, you would be very glad to hear that I have been baptised on 10 May 91 with many other pakistani people. Branch President brother Neil L. Martin baptized me and many others. The church has been growing rapidly almost all the cities in Pakistan. I hope by the grace of holy spirit in near future many will get the baptism. The rate of membership in Church is amazing, 28 members in 28 days.

Sean, I am very happy, I have received the holy Spirit, and I am ordained as Aaronic priest. I have received the Gift of the Holy Ghost. Being a Aaronic Priest I feel very happy. Although I am facing lot of problems and criticism in my community, but I know that this church is true. I believe that the Joseph Smith is the true prophet of God. I believe that the Ezra Taft Benson is our present prophet. I have started working as missionary here in pakistan. I have also recieved a video cassette and 10 book of mormon sent by you. I gave all the 10 books to the people who were very curious about the Church and they have great love for the Church. Unluckily I could not able to enjoy the video cassette because we have no video cassette recorder having NTSC system. In Pakistan pal/secam systems VCR are used. Please convey our thankfulness and love to all the donors of MOrmon Books.

I am very thankful to you for your beautiful testimony and continue guidance which I recieved first time from book of Mormon. It's because of Holy Ghost and your strong testimony that today we became Mormon in this land. Branch President said to me on my baptism day, that you are the pioneer of the church in this land. These things are very excited and beautiful. We are specially thankful to the persons who have been donated the Mormon books to our new members. Some of them are as Rodney and Lily Marshall, Jane and the George Griffiths family. Their testimonies has really touched the heart of many pakistani members. Its a great and wonderful miracle of God. I still believe that we will be able to convert many souls in the true Church of Jesus Christ of LDS.

On 25, 26 May 91, the branch president Neil L. Martin paid visit in my home with one of the strong church member Lal Khan. We spent two days together. We visit many family. The branch president appreciated and encourage the other non member. He taught them about the Doctrine and Covenants. Although our homes are very small and our surrounding area is polluted and unhealthy area, but our hearts are big, faithful and pure. We have warm feeling for this Holy Church. Since I have been baptized I have given up the tea. My brother Sabastian has given up the smoking. Similarly many members have given up all the unhealthy things. Their life have been changed. They are filled with joys.

I am sending you pictures of some of the newly baptized members. You may send photocopies of these pictures with thanks to my friend in America Provo who send me their strong testimonies in the past. Pay our best greeting to all the member who knows us specially Mr. James McWhorter, Debbie McWhorter, Jane Hamblin, Robert Hamblin, Heather Hamblin, and Hailee Hamblin. Really their testimonies and the book of Mormon has touched the hearts of many peoples here in pakistan. Although its a Islamic state but holy Ghost is working amazingly. We have arrange a programme of praying, sacrament and teaching on 1 to 4th June 91 here in Faisalabad. I hope in these day many will get the baptism, holy Ghost and Aaronic priesthood. Now I am also permitted to baptized people. It's a wonderful gift for me.

Nowadays I am teaching some of the people. They are not well educated. They are farmer, mason and laborers. They have understood the reality of the Church, and they are seeking our help and our guidance. In the next letter, I shall send you many information about the church. O.K., I end my letter with best wishes and love to all the members living near by you. Pray for the strongest faith for the new members. Many greetings from me to your family and friends in Canada and America.

Your brother in Jesus,
Stephen Anjum

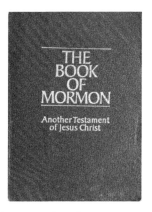

The copy of the Book of Mormon sent by Sean

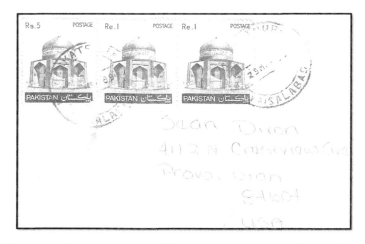

The envelope retrieved by Diane Dixon from their mailbox in the spring of 1989

APPENDIX

I know that this book is a true history. I know the book of Mormon to be true. I know that Joseph Smith was a true prophet of God. I know that he translated this book. I know that the Mormon Church is true. I hope that you will read it and pray about it and the Lord will give you a feeling that it is true.

Place Photograph Here

P.S. I'm praying for you

Name _Sean Dixon_

Address _4112 N. Crestview Provo, Utah U.S.A. 84604_

Sean Dixon's testimony, written and glued into the Book of Mormon as part of the "Family to Family" Book of Mormon program

Dear Sean,

    My name is Stephen Anjum and I am a Pakistani christain. Some times ago, I came to know about you and , (The book of Morm -on) Another Testament of Jesus Christ. I went through this Holy book and found that this is real book of God. I believe that Mor -mon Church is true, and I also Believe that Joseph Smith was a True Prophet of God. I believe that it is a gift of God . I hope that any one , who will read it and pray will get blessing of God.

    Dear Sean , I wish to be preacher of Holy Mormon . I want to get more knowledge about Mormon. Please send me some books in easy English related to Mormons . If you have any representative in Pakistan then inform me so that I may get more information from him. I hope you will accept my friendship. My mailing address is as

        C/O
        Mr. Barkat Benedict
        Standard Chartered Bank,
        Railway Road P.O Box No. 20.
        Faisalabad, Pakistan.

YOUR BROTHER IN CHRIST,
STEPHEN ANJUM,

The first letter from Stephen Anjum

Appendix

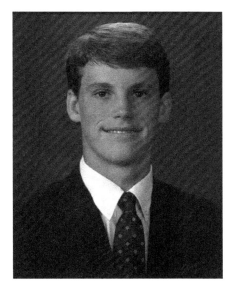

Left: Sean Dixon, age 18
Right: Stephen Anjum, age 24 (sent in his second letter to Sean)

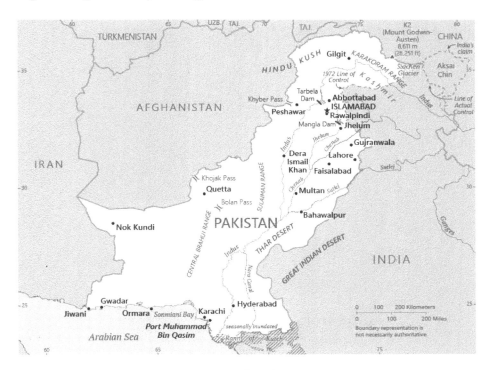

A map of Pakistan

June 22,1990

Simmons, Wilson
U.S. Embassy, Islamabad
Pakistan.

Dear Sir:
I introduce myself STEPHEN ANJUM S/O BARKAT BENEDICT from Faisalabad,Pakistan. I am member of the Mormon Church.
Since a year ago I was anxious to know the other member of the Church in Pakistan.
Recently,MERLIN R. LYBBERT, 2nd Counselor from office of the Asia Area Presidency 7 Castle Road, Hong Kong has sent me list of the members of Mormon Church in Pakistan.
I am very happy to find all of you. Really, it has given me satisfactory and happiness. Now I can share my religious terms with you and other members. I would like to know personally about you and other member in Pakistan.
I want to meet personally each member, so that I could gain more and ... knowledge about the Church. I want to go ahead in this Holy Church. I will be glad if you can spare some time for me whenever I come to Islamabad. Please let me know your residence and telephone no. so that I can contact you easily Pay my greeting and wishes to your family.

Sincerely

STEPHEN ANJUM

REDI
RESIDENCE:
        P-1042/13 , street no. 4
        waris.pura faisalabad.

Letter from Stephen to the embassy

APPENDIX

GOVERNMENT OF PAKISTAN

CERTIFICATE OF INCORPORATION

(Under section 32 of the Companies Ordinance, 1984 (XLVII of 1984)

Company Registration No. I-01826

I hereby certify that "THE CHURCH OF JESUS CHRIST OF LATTER-DAY SAINTS PAKISTAN"

is this day incorporated under the Companies Ordinance, 1984 (XLVII of 1984) and that the company is limited by Guarantee

Given under my hand at Islamabad this 11# day of October one thousand nine hundred and ninety-five

Fee Rs. 500/-(Rupees Five hundred only)

CRO-1.

(NAZIR AHMED SHAHEEN)
DEPUTY *Registrar*
of Companies
ISLAMABAD

The letter of official recognition for The Church of Jesus
Christ of Latter-day Saints in Pakistan, October 11, 1995

FROM PROVO TO PAKISTAN

We the several persons, whose names and addresses are subscribed as under are desirous of being formed into a Company in pursuance of this Memorandum of Association:-

Sr. No.	Name and Surname	Father's Name in full	Nationality with former Nationality	Occupation	Residential Address in full	Signature
1.	Daniel Siraj	Siraj Joseph	Pakistani	Service	House 50, St. 27, F-6/2, Islamabad.	
2.	Christopher Hadayat	Hadayat Masih	Pakistani	Service	Bilal Town near Dawood Nagar House 99, Street 5, Faisalabad.	
3.	Cyril West	Samuel Daniel West	Pakistani	Service	House 2, Street 7, Jinnah Park Gulberg II, Lahore.	
4.	Malcolm Adrian King	Reginald Alexander	Pakistani	Teacher	63-1/K Block 6, PECHS Karachi.	
5.	James John	John Lall Din	Pakistani	Engineer	House D-5, East Park The Mall POF Wah Cantt.	
6.	Stephen Anjum	Barkat Benedict	Pakistani	Bank Officer	House P-1042/13 Street No. 4, Warispura, Faisalabad.	
7.	Muneer Masih	Khushi Masih	Pakistani	Teacher	No. 702, Street No. 1A, Awami Colony, Lahore.	

Witness to above Signatures.

Full Name:	*Father's Name:*	*Occupation:*	*Nationality:*	*Full Address:*	*Signature*
Saleem Zulfiqar Khan	Murad Zulfiqar Khan	Bar-at-Law	Pakistani	No. 1, 2nd Floor 6-B; Markaz F-6, Islamabad.	

Dated the _____ day of _____ 1995.

The seven original signers for the official recognition of the Church in Pakistan

APPENDIX

Left: Stephen Anjum as a child with a birthmark on his leg

Right: Stephen Anjum and his parents, Barkat Benedict and Shanti Cecilia

The 1st baptism in Sialkot was 18th April, 1991 and the baptism of Stephen Anjum was 10th May, 1991

Stephen's baptism on May 10, 1991

A visit from President Jones of the Singapore Mission to the Faisalabad Branch

APPENDIX

Early Pakistani pioneers

The Faisalabad Branch (nine Pakistani people in this picture served full-time missions)

The first branch presidency of the Faisalabad Branch

Setting apart the presidency of the Faisalabad Branch

Stephen with his brothers Sabastian and Samson, all of whom became branch presidents in Faisalabad

Appendix

Left: Robert Simmons and Niels Martin teaching the early Saints

Right: Study group at the home of Stephen's father, Barkat Benedict

Left: Barkat Benedict (Stephen's father), President Niels Martin, and Stephen

Right: Stephen's uncle Patrick Pervaiz and his family—Patrick received the Book of Mormon from Stephen out in the Cholistan Desert and became a member of the first branch presidency in Karachi

APPENDIX

Stephen mentoring a young branch president in Nepal

Left: Razzaq Gill, the first missionary from Pakistan called to serve a full-time mission

Right: Razzaq Gill with his mission president in the England Birmingham Mission

Razzaq Gill and his family

Stephen and Patras Bukhari

Sean and M'Shelle Dixon wedding photo

APPENDIX

Stephen and Thomsena Anjum wedding photo

Left: The Anjum family (Stephen, Thomsena, Sharoon, and Reshayl) with the Book of Mormon
Right: Stephen and Thomsena

The Anjums and Dixons touring London

Appendix

Left: Thomsena on her marriage day
Right: Thomsena as a leader

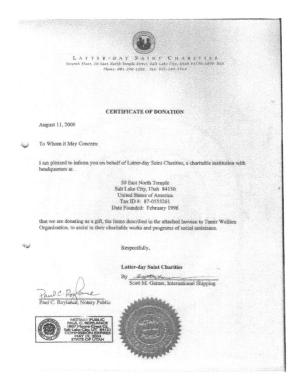

Letter of donation from LDS Charities to the Tamir Welfare Organization

The Dixons with the Anjums in London in 2006

M'Shelle and Thomsena wearing gowns made by the disabled workers in the Anjums' charity; Elder Henry Florence in the background was their host

Appendix

Left: Stephen Anjum at the London Temple

Right: The Anjum family singing "I Am a Child of God" at a fireside in the London Temple visitors' center in 2006

The Anjum family with their temple sealer, Elder Bradford, and his wife

Left: The pastor, now a friend of the Church, claps with joy as he returns the Book of Mormon to Stephen after thirty-three years

Right: Two brothers in Christ

Appendix

President and Sister Dixon as leaders of the California Redlands Mission, 2016–19

The Dixon family in 2025 (minus four grandkids and their son Scott, who was serving a mission)

The Anjum family—Sharoon, Stephen, Thomsena, and Ray

APPENDIX

Ray Anjum, Master of Cinematography

Stephen with his son Elder Sharoon Anjum
(England London Mission)

Sharoon Anjum as a student at BYU

APPENDIX

Lahore (Pakistan) District Conference, February 2023

A fireside held in Spanish Fork, Utah, with the Dixons and Anjums

Thomsena, Diane Dixon (Sean's mom), Lisie Byington, and M'Shelle wearing Pakistani gowns

Appendix

Sean and Stephen at Timpview Seminary in Provo, Utah

The Anjum family visiting the Conference Center and Church headquarters

M'Shelle, Diane Dixon (Sean's mom), Sean, Stephen, Thomsena, Sharoon, and Ray on the roof of the conference center with a fitting sign in the background (Doctrine and Covenants 133:37)

Thomsena, Stephen, and Sean with Richard Millett and the original Book of Mormon letter

Appendix

Stephen and Sean at the Dixons' mailbox

About the Authors

Sean Dixon is the director of the Utah South Institute Region for Seminaries and Institutes of Religion. He has been a seminary and institute teacher and administrator for the past thirty years. He currently is the co-host of the *Preach My Gospel* podcast, which helps pre- and post-full-time missionaries become lifelong disciples of Jesus Christ. Prior to his role at the institute, he and his wife M'Shelle presided over the California Redlands Mission from 2016 to 2019. He currently serves as a stake president in Utah. Sean has a bachelor's degree in family science and a master's degree in education. He and M'Shelle are the parents of five children and four adorable grandchildren.

In addition to his passion for teaching the gospel, Sean loves spending time with his family. He is also a big Utah Jazz and BYU sports fan. He enjoys traveling, hiking, cycling, and playing pickleball and various other sports.

Stephan Taeger is an assistant professor in ancient scripture at Brigham Young University. He received a PhD from BYU in instructional psychology and technology in 2018. His research focuses on homiletics (the study of preaching), narrative instruction, and ancient scripture.

STEPHEN ANJUM, ORIGINALLY FROM FAISALABAD, PAKISTAN, IS A COAUthor of *From Provo to Pakistan*. He was one of the first people in Pakistan to discover the Book of Mormon and initiate missionary work under the guidance of the Holy Spirit. Stephen's miraculous journey began when he encountered a personalized copy of the Book of Mormon inscribed with a testimony by Sean Dixon. This sacred text transformed Stephen's life, inspiring him to distribute hundreds of copies across Pakistan and help lay the foundation for The Church of Jesus Christ of Latter-day Saints in the country. He later served as the first branch president of the Faisalabad Branch.

In 1992, Stephen had the privilege of meeting Elder Russell M. Nelson, now President of the Church, alongside young members of the Church. They received an apostolic blessing, marking a historic moment for the Saints in Pakistan. Elder Nelson praised their faith and promised them blessings for their dedication to Christ's teachings.

Stephen cofounded Tamir Welfare Organization, a well-known charity inspired by Jesus Christ's ministry of healing. The organization serves women and children with disabilities, reflecting Christ's example of compassion and care. Registered in both Pakistan and the UK, Tamir continues to uplift vulnerable communities and fulfill its mission of service.

With a professional background spanning banking, social work, and accounting, Stephen's humanitarian efforts have taken him across Africa, Asia, Europe, and the Americas, where he has borne his testimony of the gospel. Now residing in England with his family—including his two sons, the first Latter-day Saint children born in Pakistan—Stephen remains committed to both spiritual and humanitarian service.

Stephen's story, as shared in *From Provo to Pakistan*, exemplifies the transformative power of faith, resilience, and the Book of Mormon, inspiring others to embrace the gospel of Jesus Christ.

FROM PROVO
TO PAKISTAN

FLOODING THE EARTH WITH THE BOOK OF MORMON

. an inspiring true story .